# the untold story of the
# ENTREPRENEUR'S
## wife

# PRAISE FOR *THE UNTOLD STORY OF THE ENTREPRENEUR'S WIFE*

"Amy is such a genuine soul and lovely to be around. We spent time together in a professional setting, and in a more relaxed environment, and it was obvious that she and her husband, Matt, are the real deal. *The Untold Story of the Entrepreneur's Wife* is a fantastic environment to be a part of for support, encouragement, and inspiration. Not only will you benefit from being a part of this group of like-minded, successful people, but so will your entire family."

**—Dawn Thompson,**
Keynote Speaker

"The instant I met Amy Stefanik, I was immediately impressed with her as a person, as a wife, as a mom, and as a woman deeply dedicated to helping other entrepreneurs like herself. Amy understands the struggles and challenges unique to these women—because she has lived them herself. She is clear about what these wives can do to successfully navigate this unique situation because she's had to figure out what works herself, along with her husband, Matt. Amy is super-smart, so the insights and strategies she shares are purposeful and proven. She has a huge heart; and wives that are struggling to find balance with their own entrepreneur husbands are going to find a life-saving 'light at the end of the tunnel' in Amy. I'm so excited for the lives, marriages, and families she helps to transform!"

**—Jim House**

"*The Untold Story of the Entrepreneur's Wife* is a one-of-a-kind gem, packed with practical, intuitive guidance that speaks to a unique audience. Amy Stefanik has bravely and candidly shared her journey and how she's deftly navigated it. Because she's 'been in the trenches' and has an insider's view of what it's like to be the wife of an entrepreneur, Amy speaks from the heart about what it takes to succeed in entrepreneurship, marriage, and family. Her own corporate and entrepreneurial experience, paired with a winner's spirit and firsthand knowhow, meld perfectly to make her the 'go-to authority' on how to have it all!"

**—Mary Davis,**
Author, The Entrepreneurial Mom, & Keynote Speaker

"Amy Stefanik has created an amazing movement by honoring and supporting the women who stand behind their entrepreneurial husbands. Often, it's the entrepreneur's wife who is the unsung hero, supporting her husband's dreams and realizing she shares his attentions and affection for his business. My wife has been the backbone behind my success and I couldn't have done it without her. I was honored to be able to honor her."

**—Brad Costanzo,**
Costanzo Marketing

"I am absolutely thrilled to see a project like *The Untold Story of the Entrepreneur's Wife*! Coming from an entertainment and entrepreneurial background, and now married to an entrepreneur, I love that there is a platform that reveals and sheds light on the truth of what it takes to not only *start* on this journey, but also on the everyday commitment it takes to *stay* on this journey for all those involved. *The Untold Story of the Entrepreneur's Wife* highlights the sacrifices made to have the life of 'freedom' as an entrepreneur, as well as provides a space to be heard and understood for those in the forefront and in the shadows."

**—Michelle Inez Castaldi Mann**

# the untold story of the
# ENTREPRENEUR'S
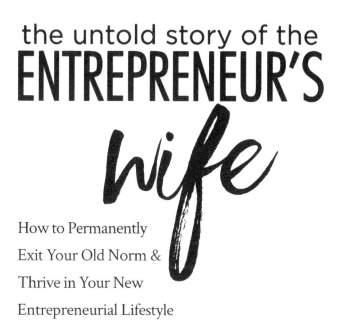
*wife*

How to Permanently
Exit Your Old Norm &
Thrive in Your New
Entrepreneurial Lifestyle

# AMY STEFANIK

NEW YORK

LONDON • NASHVILLE • MELBOURNE • VANCOUVER

# The Untold Story of the Entrepreneur's Wife

## How to Permanently Exit Your Old Norm and Thrive in Your New Entrepreneurial Lifestyle

Published in New York, New York, by Morgan James Publishing in partnership with Difference Press. Morgan James is a trademark of Morgan James, LLC. www.MorganJamesPublishing.com

The Morgan James Speakers Group can bring authors to your live event. For more information or to book an event visit The Morgan James Speakers Group at www.TheMorganJamesSpeakersGroup.com.

ISBN 9781642790801 paperback
ISBN 9781642790818 eBook
Library of Congress Control Number: 2018943175

| **Cover Design by:** | **Interior Design by:** |
|---|---|
| Megan Dillon | Christopher Kirk |
| megan@creativeninjadesigns.com | www.GFSstudio.com |

In an effort to support local communities, raise awareness and funds, Morgan James Publishing donates a percentage of all book sales for the life of each book to Habitat for Humanity Peninsula and Greater Williamsburg.

Get involved today! Visit
www.MorganJamesBuilds.com

*"Don't dig up in doubt what you planted in Faith"*

*—Elizabeth Elliot*

**To my husband, *Matt Stefanik***

*Without you encouraging me to reach my goals,*
*I could not have made it here.*

*Thank you for always being my biggest fan.*

*We have been through a lot of amazing adventures together,*

*and I believe it is still only the beginning.*

# CONTENTS

# GRATEFUL THANKS

To all my many friends that have supported, believed in, and encouraged me throughout the process of sharing my story.

While it's impossible to list each person that has impacted me along this road, I'd like to name a few that have propelled me forward and created the space for me to build *The Untold Story of the Entrepreneur's Wife.*

### Special thanks to
Brad Costanzo

Kenia Martins Costa

Sean Stephenson

Mindie Kniss

Jim House

Alex Charfen

Cadey Charfen

James Malinchak

Jason Goldberg

Jeremiah Baker

Mira Mambetalieva

Tabitha Larsson

# FOREWORD

EVERY ONCE IN a while, a book comes along that can truly change your life. Amy Stefanik has written that book. As an entrepreneur, you're never taught how to handle the challenging times that often come with the entrepreneur life. You're never taught how to make sure your family is always a top priority and never feels neglected. Amy is on a mission to help solve that challenge.

*The Untold Story of the Entrepreneur's Wife* is a book that has been needed for years. It provides ideas and real-life examples of how to maneuver through the unknown that an entrepreneur's family often faces while the entrepreneur is on their journey of building their business!

Read this book, then read it again because Amy Stefanik's ideas will change your life! This is a must read for all entrepreneurs around the world!

**—Kevin Harrington**
Original Shark on the Hit TV Show, *Shark Tank*
Inventor of the Infomercial
($5 Billion in Sales)

# PREFACE

DURING THE PAST fifteen years, I've been on a unique journey that's still continuing today. The entrepreneur's wife's journey is one that comes with no roadmap, cannot be charted by any GPS, and one for which no instruction manual exists. As I've traveled, there have been rocky roads, potholes, dangerous cliffs, unexpected detours, and maybe even a few unfortunate pedestrian casualties along the way. Throughout my journey as the entrepreneur's wife, I've had to take an introspective look at myself, face my ego, and even question my purpose, both in the journey and in life.

The most valuable lessons I've learned during my journey were not discovered on the highest mountain peaks, during the good and easy times. They were unearthed, like treasured artifacts, in the darkest of valleys where I'd come to rest, exhausted, overwhelmed, and ready to end my journey—or at least take a detour toward the unknown.

In the early years, I was usually a passenger on my journey, along for the ride and not intent on taking the helm and steering. While this arrangement might work in some instances, it is not without its repercussions. The problem with being pushed around by the hands of the universe is that it makes us become hardened to what's around us and to the possibilities that await. It makes it difficult to stay focused on the reason we first began our journey.

When Matt and I first began our journey together, I had my own big dreams too; and so, I took the plunge and started a business of my own. We ignored the naysayers, those that didn't understand the entrepreneurial mindset that compels business owners to set off on their own in search of freedom and their own visions of success. We dug in, worked hard, compromised, and made some sacrifices like all business owners must do at times. Before long, we began to see the fruits of our labor, and we started to reap the rewards of our efforts. It had been a predictable cause and effect scenario, and the way things should work out for those willing to put in the hard work.

But when the real estate market crashed, all the hard work in the world couldn't stop the downward spiral in which we were ensnared. Matt and I were both in the passenger's seat by this time as we lost his business, three houses, our cars, and any sense of security that we'd amassed. Along with our material possessions, I also gave up my business and my dreams. Those naysayers knowingly shook their heads and offered-up empty 'I told you so' comments as we scrambled to salvage the pieces of our life and our shattered dreams for the future. Defeated and beaten, we packed up the fragments of our lives and moved our children to a different state in hopes of starting over.

The fall from those heights left me frightened to step outside the box again and scared even to let myself dare to dream. So, I didn't. I protectively walled up my box, carefully stayed within its sturdy walls, and played it safe. I got a job, created a career within corporate America, and silenced the voice inside me that had once been my guide, my cheerleader, and my trusted confidante. I carefully colored within the lines and mechanically did my part in our predictable life as Matt and I tried to rebuild our world.

Fast-forward six years and Matt had rebuilt his empire; we'd climbed out of the ruins, brushed ourselves off, and once again found financial freedom. But although I'd pulled myself from the rubble, the wounds were still there, evidence of the injuries and pain I'd suffered. Although I outwardly functioned, I was paralyzed inside. I ignored an inner voice that urged me to get moving, answer my calling, and live up to my potential in this life.

We'd been so busy and so focused on getting Matt's vision off the ground that it soon became impossible for me to even hear my inner voice anymore. But when we ignore the universe, bad things can happen. In my case, I got sick. Not the coughing, feverish sickness, but mentally, I was not my best self. Hurt and resentment took root inside me, and I stopped believing in what could be, in the future, in the possibilities. I ceased to dream. If even a thought of 'what if' seeped into my mind, I cringed and pushed it away. I didn't dare allow myself to dream of what could be. I'd been beaten down and wounded, and I was in a self-protection mode as if my life depended on it.

Years earlier, Matt and I had looked at impressive, multi-million-dollar homes, and together we dreamed of what we'd do in the future when we'd found success. But now, I no longer wanted to even play the fantasy game. What was the point? The negative dialog played incessantly inside my head and reminded me that there was no time for dreaming. It was a useless luxury, one that I could no longer afford.

My lackluster desire to think big was frustrating to Matt. To him, it seemed that I was disappearing, the light inside me dimming. He did his best to reach me, but nothing worked. Our paths were dividing and leading us further away from one another, as he felt like I no longer believed in him or his dreams. We had arguments about how I was one of his 'haters' and he told me that if I didn't solve my current issues they'd become bigger problems down the road when he'd become successful. In his mind, 'if I wasn't with him, then I was against him,' and nothing I did or said showed him otherwise. Instead of it being 'us against the world,' it had become 'us against each other.'

Our mindsets had shifted, and we'd started to unravel. Matt threw himself into rebuilding his world, but he didn't feel the support of his wife. I withdrew into myself and emotionally shut down, almost in a hibernation-like, self-preservation method. I felt that if I 'didn't fully participate' that I couldn't get hurt or disappointed again. If I didn't get in the game, then I couldn't lose the game. But I was robotically giving and giving, as best I could in my desperate state, yet I didn't stop to refill my tank. I'd sometimes become upset, but have no idea as to why, and I felt uncomfortable and uneasy in my own skin. I didn't realize it at the time, but I needed to get to a place where my inner light was brighter than my own ego. Being unfulfilled was eating me up from the inside, destroying my inner soul a bit at a time.

As Matt began to have successes again, I didn't feel angry or resentful toward him or his earned success, but rather it made me angry that I was facing my own disappointments and lack of personal success. The separation between us was incredibly painful to me because I wasn't a 'hater' at all. I was hurting and feeling unfulfilled. Our battle, and my internal struggle, continued and festered for several years. The lack of communication and lack of giving on both sides grew into an ugly, poisonous monster that threatened to annihilate us.

Even though I'd found much success in my corporate career, and Matt's businesses were thriving, we were miserable as a couple. We were on top again, from a financial perspective, and Matt was making a nice six-figure salary, but our marriage was stuck. Our journey couldn't continue, and there was even the possibility that we'd slide backwards since neither of us was putting in the effort to keep the marriage going. We were at a crossroad and decisions had to be made before either of us could go on. The road looked different to us now, and the gray fog that hung over us made it difficult to see which way to go.

Anger, resentment, and frustration had worn on us like water steadily erodes a rock, and it had nearly torn us apart. As we stood at the crossroad in our journey, we had to decide whether to stay together or go our separate ways. We were an entrepreneurial family that had been so intent on focusing on success, power, and creating a certain lifestyle, that we'd forgotten to tend our relationship, the very thing that had led us to the journey in the first place.

It's so easy to get distracted and to throw our energies into our businesses or careers, the things that make us money and support our families. We tend our businesses, we go to great lengths to maintain clients, we put in tremendous effort to cultivate new customers, we nurture our professional relationships, and yet it's easy to forget to tend the nucleus and the heart of it all: our marriage. But business is not the only valuable thing that needs developing and nurturing.

Think about this for a minute: If you work twenty-four hours a day and put all your efforts into the hustle, you will most likely become very successful. But what is success if you one day get to the finish line, but your family is no longer there? All the success and money in the world will mean nothing. Your bank account might be full, but your heart will be empty when you realize your family became a casualty of the grind and the hustle.

My journey has affirmed for me that sometimes we must be completely broken and humbled, to the point of falling on our knees before God, to rebuild and redirect our life's path. If only we ask, God will help us to steer ourselves back onto the road, and after we do the necessary work, He will even lead us to the point where our lives can intersect and once again become one.

Entrepreneurs are a unique set of people, defined by how they approach life, coupled with an unstoppable work ethic and a desire to succeed. If we treat our marriages with the same enthusiasm, dedication, curiosity, belief, and hustle that we dedicate to our business, our relationship can also be highly successful. That doesn't mean everything will always be sunshine and roses. There will still be some cloudy days. Just like with business, sometimes marriage can be tough, challenging, exhausting, and unpredictable. But we'd do almost anything to salvage our business. So, shouldn't we put the same effort and dedication into our marriage?

Why is it that people will refuse to give up on their dreams of entrepreneurial success, and yet they'll throw up their hands in defeat and walk away from marital commitments? It's natural that we are loyal to our business partners, associates, and customers, and yet we may still waiver when it comes to morals and responsibilities to our spouse. It's so easy to allow our lives to become very one-sided and self-driven, but when that happens, a profound imbalance occurs. So, are we entirely successful if parts of our lives are failing and falling apart?

As hard as it was for Matt to professionally climb back to the top, the endeavor was nothing compared to the battle he and I faced when we'd finally began to climb back to one another. Unfortunately, many things had to happen before I could gain clarity and steel myself for the hard work that lay ahead. I am so grateful that in my darkest of times, when I reached out to God in desperation, that He answered and helped to illuminate the road He wanted us to take.

Because I've walked through the pain and done harder work than I've ever done in my career or my business, I share my story to help other entrepreneurial couples and families. Let me be clear that I don't wish to portray a false sense of perfection and that in no way are Matt and I perfect. We faced divorce because of a lack of understanding and an unwillingness to bend our egos. We've been beaten up along our journey, and we'll always have the battle scars to prove it, but today, I'm proud of those scars because they remind me that I fought for what was most important. I believe we went through hell so that we can help others who are going through some of the same obstacles and roadblocks we faced.

Today I passionately write, coach, lead, and teach about hard work, positive mindsets, and always being a work in progress—and I'm not talking about how we manage our business! The entrepreneurial journey is not for the weak, but together, as a team, it is easier to bear and so much more gratifying and fulfilling. If you've got a team worth fighting for, then I want to share with you my playbook of how we won the fight—together!

*"She stood in the storm, and when the wind did not
blow her way, she adjusted her sails."*

—Elizabeth Edwards

# A MINDSET SHIFT

# 1

# IN THE BEGINNING

OUR STORY STARTED like many others when Matt and I were introduced to one another by a mutual friend that happened to be my neighbor. At age twenty, I'd just gotten out of a long, somewhat tumultuous relationship, and so, at the time, I didn't want to get into a serious relationship. A Florida girl my whole life, I'd grown up in Lakeland, a city west of Orlando once known for its citrus crops, first planted by the earliest settlers in the mid-1800's. It was a place where people were often born and raised, and they married one another and started their own families, an area where everyone knew everyone.

Originally from Ohio, Matt was twenty-one and a college basketball player. He had come to attend the University of South Florida in Tampa, about a half-hour's drive from where I lived. When we first met, it was a bit awkward. But as Matt talked about his desire to get into real estate, I became intrigued by this northern guy's visions for his future. It was my first glimpse that Matt wanted to be an entrepreneur.

The next weekend was our first date, a group date really, and Matt and I joined friends for dinner and drinks. I found myself drawn to the good-looking, dark-haired guy that was so different from the boys I'd grown up around. The more he talked, the more I realized Matt's visions were much broader than the hunter-type outdoorsy guys I'd known. I loved his energy and the way he saw the world as a huge place filled with opportunity for anyone willing to get a piece of it. Although I couldn't identify it at the time, Matt had an entrepreneurial mindset, and as handsome as he was, I was especially drawn to his positivity and his desire to succeed. It was like he recognized the endless possibilities that awaited him, if only he worked for them.

When we first met, Matt and I both lived in apartments, and we each had a roommate. I also had a sweet one-year-old daughter, whose father I had married as soon as I'd graduated high school. Divorced for just six months when I met Matt, I was a young, single mother, much to the chagrin of my traditional parents who would celebrate their fiftieth wedding anniversary a few years later. Mom and Dad felt that marriage was 'for life.' Although I'd known my daughter's father since we were both thirteen, everyone agreed that I'd made an error in judgment when I married him just after high school.

As the youngest of their seven children, Mom and Dad were concerned for my future as a single mother, but they were equally enamored with their granddaughter, a constant fixture in their lives. Raised in a strict Christian family, my values were instilled at a young age and reinforced throughout my life, and I knew I'd raise my daughter in the same way. Maybe those values were the catalyst for my decision to leave my husband when I didn't like how our relationship began changing. Whatever the reason, I was glad I did since it led to the opportunity to date Matt.

The more I knew him, the more I liked him. After six months, Matt and I decided to live together in Sarasota, located on the southwestern coast of Florida and at the southern end of Tampa Bay. About half the size of Lakeland, Sarasota is an area known for cultural events, beaches, and resorts. It is also home to the famed Ringling circus family's palatial mansion that stands as testament to the American Dream. Little did I know that Matt and I were on the cusp of building our own version of the American Dream too.

After we'd settled into our apartment together, Matt and I began our journey. I got a job as a personal assistant to a female corporate executive and Matt was just getting into flipping houses. When I wasn't working, I rode along with Matt as he canvassed neighborhoods one street at a time in search of houses that he could flip.

"Tell me exactly what we're looking for," I said.

"Opportunity!" he grinned.

Matt drove, and I wrote information on a yellow legal pad in my lap. What we were looking for were houses that looked vacant or unkempt. Sometimes they had dead lawns, newspapers piled up in the driveway, peeling paint, broken exterior lights, and overgrown trees and shrubs. But they couldn't have been more beautiful to Matt because he saw the potential in them! He saw the opportunity to flip them and make a profit.

After hours and hours of scouting for properties, we took our list of possibilities and headed home. Using the internet, Matt then looked up the owners of the homes, using the properties' physical addresses. His next step was to contact those owners.

"Sir, you don't know me, but I was driving by a home you own today, and I noticed it looks like it's vacant. If you'd be interested in selling it in 'as is' condition, I'd like to talk to you," he'd tell the owners.

Many times, those owners were relieved that anyone had taken the time to track them down. Sometimes their homes had been rental properties and their tenants had destroyed the houses and skipped out on their leases. A few were homes that had been owned by older people who were deceased, so their homes were left vacant, just waiting for their heirs to sell the properties. There were a few homes whose owners had moved but had been unable to repair their properties, and therefore, the houses just sat untended and deteriorated in the Florida sun. Some homes had once been occupied by retirees that had since moved in with their families or got into other living arrangements, which meant their houses hadn't been maintained.

Sometimes there were liens on the homes that had to be satisfied and even some unpaid utilities that needed to be paid. But these were minor details that could be taken care of at the real estate closings so that the clear title could transfer to the homes' new owners. In most cases, the neighbors in the surrounding neighborhoods were thrilled that someone had purchased the 'forgotten' homes since they needed repairs and maintenance and created unkempt eyesores that affected property values all around. It was a 'win-win' situation for all concerned. The homeowners were happy to be paid for their properties in 'as is' condition, so they didn't have any cash outlay, the mortgage companies got paid, liens were sometimes satisfied, contractors got paid for repairing the houses, so they'd sell, and Matt made his profits as he flipped each home to its new buyer.

At first, Matt used investors or OPM (other people's money) to broker the deals. They made money, and he made money. It was a good system, and Matt developed a system as he found and flipped properties again and again. The real estate market was good at the time, and Matt was good at what he did. Again, it was a perfect combination for success.

Everyone, however, did not share our exuberance or our vision, nor did they understand the entrepreneurial mindset. Some people thought that if my husband wasn't working a typical nine-to-five grind that he somehow wasn't gainfully employed. It was as if they felt that since someone else wasn't writing him a paycheck, that it was impossible for him to make a living wage.

"When's he going to a job?" they'd ask.

"He needs to look for stable employment, so he can provide for his family," some said.

"What about health insurance? He needs an employer, so he can get benefits."

"That house flipping stuff is fine as a sideline, but a husband needs a real job, so he can take care of his wife and kids."

While I realized that entrepreneurship is not for everyone, I'll admit that it really irked me that some people just couldn't see the big picture. I didn't feel that I needed to defend my husband's decisions, especially since it was becoming more and more obvious that he was having success with what he was doing. It was as if the cynics needed to feel like they knew more than others, as they played it safe with their traditional jobs. I even wondered if a couple of them wanted to see Matt fail, just so they could triumphantly declare 'I told you so.'

But I quieted my boiling irritation, and I continued to steadfastly support my man and his decisions, like any good spouse would and should do. For entrepreneurs, it can sometimes feel like being alone on an island, but it's also a great feeling when they can later buy that whole island! That tangible barometer of success is just one of the pay-offs entrepreneurs seek. Yet it's an inconceivable notion to people who aren't wired with an entrepreneur's mentality.

> *"Be an encourager.*
> *The world has plenty of critics already."*
> —*Dave Willis*

One night, Matt talked to me about a house he'd found and the potential he felt it held to make a nice net profit. After I had put my daughter to bed, I went to the living room to talk with him about the house.

"The only thing," Matt said, "Is that the owner is in Canton, Ohio. But I just know that if I can get in front of him, and talk to him, that I can get the house under contract."

It was a pivotal moment for me, and one I'd always remember. Matt's determination and will to succeed was infectious. I wanted to support him and to see him reach his goals.

"Well then, let's drive to Ohio in the morning!" I said, fully in support of the man I loved and the dream he envisioned.

Matt liked that I was his 'ride or die chick,' the person that had all the faith in the world in him and his abilities. At the time, I was making just $275 a week and we didn't have extra money in the bank in those days. If we wasted my paycheck, the loss would be huge and painful. It would mean the difference in paying our bills and even buying groceries. Just the thought of using a week's pay to fund our road trip took a gigantic leap of faith! We didn't have money to spare! But we had hope, we had a dream, and we had a determination to succeed and to build our future. When we decided to take the risk, it proved to be a pivotal, life-altering moment.

While Matt had grown up in Ohio, it was the first time this Florida girl had ever seen snow as we pulled into Canton. He dropped me at his mother's home, and then he eagerly went to talk to the man that owned the abandoned home in Florida.

"Uh, no, no," the man said, as Matt stood on his frozen doorstep. "I'm not ready to talk about selling that place."

"Sir, I've just driven sixteen hours, just to come and talk to you," Matt said. "Will you just give me five minutes of your time?" An hour later, Matt returned to his mother's house.

"I got it!" he grinned, as he waved a signed contract in the air.

That moment was the first time that I saw 'the entrepreneurial spark,' and Matt's excitement was infectious! He wasn't excited about purchasing the house; he was excited about the opportunities and the prospects of what he could do with it. This girl from Lakeland, Florida was exhilarated to witness how Matt had taken an idea, acted upon it, and followed his faith to create his own destiny!

Failure simply was not an option at the time—for many reasons. Matt didn't even entertain the fact that his plans might not work, and it was a good thing he felt so strongly because we had very little cash in the bank in those days. Before we left Ohio, Matt had the seller sign a power of attorney that allowed Matt to speak directly to the bank about the property on the seller's behalf. The seller was glad to do it because it made the sale even simpler, and less time-consuming for him too.

• • •

As Matt grew his business, our relationship grew too. He was great with my daughter. In fact, he'd been the other father she'd known and I was grateful to have him in her life. In time, Matt and I married, and we both looked toward the future with excitement. It was 2004, and the real estate market was providing a great life for us, with no end in sight.

After he'd flipped houses for a couple of years, Matt took a partner. Together, they arranged cash deals for the houses they bought and sold, each time rolling their profits into their next deal. Matt had, by now, fine-tuned his process for locating, obtaining, renovating, and selling the properties he flipped. It was so gratifying to watch him as he turned his visions into realities and followed his dreams.

# *2*
# BUILDING A LIFE

MATT CONTINUED WORKING his system, and we began to build our life and our family together. I left my job with the corporate executive for a job at a local animal hospital, and in time, I learned that I was pregnant. After working through most of my pregnancy, I decided to quit my job just before our son would be born in 2005. Matt and I planned that I'd stay home with the children since his business was going so well.

Shortly after our son was born, we bought our first home together for our growing family. But I'd watched as Matt had built his business and grown his dreams, and I wanted to feel that entrepreneurial excitement that comes with creating one's own success. When our son was nearly a year old, I decided to start my own business.

"What type of business?" Matt asked. "What are you thinking?"

I explained that my ex-sister-in-law had done well with her Mary Kay business.

"She brought me onboard," I told Matt. "But at the time, I simply bought my samples case, but then, I didn't do a thing with it. I was what they called 'a pink peddler.' But I'm at a different point in my life now, so I think I'm up for the challenge."

Matt supported my decision, and he understood my yearning to create my own success. I didn't want to contact my ex-sister-in-law though, and I preferred to start anew with another consultant. She immediately put me in contact with her Mary Kay Director whom I soon met for coffee. The more the Director talked, the more I felt sure that it was something I wanted to do. The income potential sounded wonderful, but I also had a genuine desire to help women feel good about themselves.

"You'll sign an agreement with the company," the consultant explained. "And then, you can purchase your inventory and get started!"

I plunged full force into my entrepreneurial endeavor, purchasing $1,800 of inventory. I had big goals—and no intention of not meeting them. I hardly knew anyone in Sarasota, but I committed to myself that I'd talk to anyone and everyone about the benefits of Mary Kay. Potential customers were everywhere! Malls, restaurants, schools, hair salons, playgrounds, and kids' birthday parties were just a few of the areas where I found my customers.

One afternoon, as I shopped for groceries, I got an idea. I 'accidentally' dropped a cucumber in the produce aisle and a nice woman said 'Here, let me get that for you!' as she stooped to retrieve it.

"Oh! Thanks so much!" I smiled. "That's so nice of you! Hey, listen, I'm a Mary Kay consultant, and I'd love to give you a facial sometime!"

That 'thank you facial' turned into a full-blown Mary Kay party at the woman's home and I sold lots of product to nice women, several of whom booked their own parties for later dates. A few more ladies became regular customers too.

I truly enjoyed what I was doing. I met countless nice women and had the opportunity to positively impact how they felt about themselves. Some of them had been having bad days when we met, or they just didn't 'feel pretty' or 'didn't feel confident.' With a genuine heart and a caring spirit—plus some amazing Mary Kay products—I positively impacted many women. It felt great to watch as ladies transformed themselves, walked a little taller, and smiled a little brighter! I wasn't just selling makeup; I was providing opportunity and possibilities for these women. In some cases, that's all it took to give them the boost their lives had been needing!

In only five months, I'd earned my first Mary Kay car, a red Pontiac Vibe. That shiny new car sat proudly in my driveway, testament to my rapid-fire success and evidence that I was doing well in my business! It felt awesome to be creating my own prosperity, and I loved the fact that ours was a two-entrepreneur home! Matt and I had the world at our fingertips, and our appetites had been whetted for more! The harder we worked, the better we did! It was the perfect example of how entrepreneurs control their destinies, and we were living proof that we had what it takes.

Two months after I'd earned my car, I became a Sales Director, which meant I had thirty people under me. My entrepreneurial journey had picked up speed and I was speeding toward more success than even I'd imagined! Even with thirty people under me, I continued to do home parties too. I regularly filled my car's trunk with Mary Kay's familiar pink-packaged products, and I did in-home parties. Sure, I was selling products, and 'sales' was the end-goal, but I also enjoyed what I was doing.

Once a month, I held a meeting in my own home for the thirty ladies that were underneath me in our region. Not only were these meetings social gatherings, but they were opportunities to introduce new products, talk about selling techniques, and share things. Let's be honest: women are great talkers, and we appreciate valuable information!

We all looked forward to these get-togethers; and I made sure everyone went away feeling motivated and excited about working hard for the next month and then coming together again to celebrate our successes. Sometimes during my parties, my toddler son was in his bedroom, with a baby gate at the door, and he peeked his little head out to see what all the women were laughing at in the living room. But this was fine with everyone, since most of the ladies were also mothers too who had kids of their own.

As I grew my Mary Kay business, it seemed like the sky was the limit! When we find our passion, and plunge into it with all we've got, we can't help but make it a success! I was running my own business, controlling my destiny, and steering my life's journey—and Matt was doing the same thing. We made an unstoppable duo!

• • •

The real estate market continued to thrive at a time when banks were writing loans for almost anyone with a pulse, whether they could afford the mortgage payments and terms or not. The atmosphere felt charged with electricity at that time. Real estate changed hands at a rapid pace and banks loaned money on new loans before the ink had even dried on the previous ones. But what was brewing just below the surface was like the storm of the century, and something no one had seen since 1929.

Somehow though, when we're in a situation, it's difficult to step back and get a broad perspective. Had we had an inkling of where life would take us, we'd have prepared ourselves and made different, more conservative decisions.

For the first couple months of 2008, it felt like there was a calm status quo. Banks continued to update uneasy investors and assure them that their money was safe. Homebuyers continued to purchase their pieces of the American Dream, secure that since bankers had approved them, they could afford their mortgages and the terms of their loans. Although those at the helm of the banking system most likely saw the storm brewing on the horizon, hard-working folks like us just continued doing what we'd been doing, as we worked to build the life we desired.

But the house of cards wasn't as stable as we'd thought, and we didn't have the control that we'd imagined. When bad news hits Wall Street, it seems so far away, and like it can't touch the typical working class. We hear about it on the news, while we're cooking dinner, but it doesn't seem like it's in the kitchen with us, like it can permeate the safety of our home's walls. But just the opposite is true, and the decisions of those at the helm would have a rapid, trickle-down effect on people that needed their money the most.

As rumor that a banking collapse was imminent, people grew nervous. Matt and I had been so excited about the life we were building, and we thought that no matter what happened, we could hang on until the economic climate stabilized again. But we didn't have as much control as we thought. Banks, insurance companies, and the real estate market were in trouble—and so were we.

*"The meaning of life is to find your gift. The purpose of life is to give it away."*

*— Pablo Picasso*

# 3
# A CHANGING CLIMATE

A S THE FIRST signs of trouble began to emerge, Matt and I tried to stay positive and remain focused. Things started to get shaky as banks were forced to make loans in subprime areas as things began to shift. After loaning money to anyone and everyone, sometimes even for 100 percent or more of a home's value, investors began to get scared and banks tightened their belts. Eventually, when banks realized they'd have to absorb the losses when their borrowers' 'too good to pass up loans' came due, they scrambled to sell off what they could of their 'toxic, devalued assets.' When money had been readily available, housing prices had increased, but when sellers couldn't find qualified buyers, housing prices began to fall... and fall... and fall. The housing bubble had burst, and the ripple effect was felt like aftershocks of a cata-strophic earthquake. This time, when news of the banking and real estate crash was on the TV, it was 'art imitating life,' and we were stuck in the middle of the implosion with the fallout all around us.

Matt and I had always made things work in the past. Hard work and dedication had paved our way to a better life. But now, things weren't only in our control. Matt continued to try to sell the homes he'd prepared to flip, while I continued as a Sales Director with Mary Kay. It became difficult though to put on a smile and portray a positive 'can do' attitude to the ladies that were underneath me. I felt like a fraud as I talked about how awesome the 'Mary Kay way' was—not because Mary Kay is not fantastic, but because the rest of my life was falling apart. People saw a perfectly coiffed, manicured, sharply-dressed woman. Underneath the mastery of makeup lay a frightened, nervous, uncertain woman that didn't really have control of her destiny.

I was sure Matt was tired of my constant rhetorical question of 'What are we going to do?' When I vocalized my own fears, it only served to validate Matt's fears that he'd tried to suppress in his attempt to remain positive. The negativity became infectious, and there was no good in it.

We had three houses, and all the carrying costs that go along with that, plus, we had two children, Matt's car payment, the usual household bills, and ever-mounting expenses. As much as we hated to do it, we were forced to borrow from family and friends. We even started selling off some of our furniture to make ends meet. For about a year, we hung on like this. It was not a good feeling for either one of us.

"Why doesn't Matt go and get a job?" some of my family asked.

No one ever asked such questions when times were good and we were doing well. I felt like I had to defend my husband and his decisions. In time though, such comments began to validate the gremlins in my head, those little chattering voices that infected me with doubts and questions. As I continued with my Mary Kay business, I grew dubious about our future.

With just three more payments left on Matt's Mitsubishi Galant, we couldn't come up with the funds to make it, but we absolutely couldn't ask our friends or family for another loan. When the tow truck finally came for the car, our neighbors stood in front of their homes and watched as our car was repossessed. As the driver pulled away, he took a piece of our pride, along with the car, and we were incredibly humiliated. Thankfully, I still had my Mary Kay car that we could drive for transportation.

• • •

I felt depressed when we decided to go and visit a friend in Lakeland. The thought of talking and laughing with people didn't even seem possible. It was difficult to put one foot in front of the other, just to keep going. We met some new people at my friend's home, and as we talked, one of them said, "You know, North Carolina's housing market is pretty stable."

Matt and I have always believed in signs, and we'd been asking for a sign and searching for answers about what to do. We agreed that maybe we were meant to hear this and to take it as a suggestion of what to do next. We began to talk to people and research the housing market in North Carolina.

By this time, I was in the 'fight or flight' mode, so I was ripe for a change.

I found a rental home in Ramseur, North Carolina, a small town located about sixty miles outside of Greensboro. The two-story house wasn't huge, but it looked nice. Matt and I felt like it would be a fresh start for us.

"We can do this," I said. "You'll get into real estate, and I'll do Mary Kay in the area. We can make it work."

We had a plan and a new direction. Matt and I felt hopeful that we'd rebuild and move forward in life.

Back in Florida, we sold everything to make the move to North Carolina. We even sold our baby's crib, as much as we hated to let it go. It was painful to sell our baby's bed. It somehow signified that we'd hit rock bottom and been left with no other choices but to release something that held such cherished memories. Our daughter was by this time in kindergarten and our son was two years old. To them, our move seemed like a big family adventure. To us, it seemed like our only choice.

We drove through pouring rain for the last part of our trip. It was still a gloomy, gray day when we pulled up to our new home. Matt and I were disappointed to see that the sellers had left the house in such a horrific state. No attempt to clean had been made, inside or out, and remnants of the previous owners lay everywhere, just waiting to be cleaned up, spruced up, or hauled away. It felt like I'd been kicked in the stomach and I began to cry. Deep, guttural sobs wracked my trembling body.

"How much more can we take?" I cried, as Matt tried to comfort me.

He held me, as we were surrounded by dirty walls that bore reminders of the sellers' dirty, black dogs that had leaned on every available space in the house. It was a depressing 'welcome home,' to say the least. We'd had so many sleepless nights in recent months, plus we were exhausted from the physical and mental stress of the move. I'm sure that was part of the reason for my meltdown, but in the moment, I was overwhelmed and I felt defeated.

"It'll be okay," Matt said. "Listen, this is just a part of our story."

"We are not putting our children in this house until it's been cleaned," I said. "It's disgusting in here!"

"Let's go to a hotel for tonight, and we can come back tomorrow morning and clean it," he agreed.

That's how it usually was with us. When one of us melted down, the other knew to be strong and stay positive. We knew we both couldn't fall apart at the same time. I've always been the quick-triggered, more anxious one, while Matt is the calmer, more even keel sort. Some might say we each balance the other. Perhaps we each see something in the other that's different from ourselves and that's what first drew us together. Whatever the answer, it's a precarious balancing act at times, but it works for us.

Matt got back into the U-Haul truck, and I got into my Mary Kay Vibe, ready to follow the truck. But we weren't going anywhere soon. The heavy moving truck was stuck in the mud in the front yard of our new home.

"What next?" I cried, as I pounded my steering wheel in frustration.

We got some help and got the truck freed from the mud, and then we finally headed to a nearby hotel for the night. The next morning, we returned to the house with cleaning products and a rented carpet shampooer. The seller had been nearly impossible to deal with, so it wasn't so surprising that the house was in such a horrific state. It was disappointing though, because we hadn't left our homes in Florida in the same disrespected, filthy state, but I suppose people have different standards and expectations.

Matt and I worked hard to clean and paint the house and turn it into a home for our family. We tried to stay positive about rebuilding our life as we looked toward the future. Even surrounded by the new paint on the walls, I don't think I truly grasped that I'd have to 'start over from scratch' in our new town. In Florida, I'd steadily grown my Mary Kay network, and I had built a strong foundation of reps and customers. But without me there in person to motivate and push them, the reps' sales figures slid. Sure, I could have started from nothing and built a new network of Mary Kay reps in North Carolina, but I didn't have the energy.

What I did have was a ton of Mary Kay products, since I'd moved my inventory to our new home. In Florida, I'd stored my inventory in floor-to-ceiling cabinets, so I had a LOT of product to liquidate! Feeling beaten and defeated, I decided to step down from my position of Sales Director with Mary Kay. Essentially, I gave up on my dream.

I placed ads on several sites and sold off my products. Little by little, as my inventory left, I watched my dreams dissolve. I withdrew into myself and became numb. It was my coping mechanism at the time, and one I resorted to when left with no other options. In my mind, if I was numb then I couldn't feel, and if I couldn't feel, then I couldn't hurt.

In time, Matt and I purchased a second car, so we had car payments again, but we also had a second form of transportation, a necessity for a busy, young family. We'd presumed Mary Kay would send someone to retrieve the car, but we also chose to ignore the inevitable. One afternoon, as we drove home, a flatbed truck approached us, coming from the opposite direction. On it, chained to the flatbed, sat my prized red Vibe, the only remaining proof of my previous success with Mary Kay, and the last tangible evidence of my entrepreneurial achievements.

"They came for my car!" I said as the flatbed passed us.

It felt like the door to my past success had slammed shut with a resounding finality that echoed 'failure' inside my head. But I knew I couldn't dwell on it. There was no time to waste energy on dwelling on things I couldn't change. I knew I had to keep pushing forward, so I stuffed down my feelings and locked them deep inside of myself.

Matt had started doing foreclosure inspections and preparing bank-owned homes for winterizing, a reality that's virtually unknown to Floridians, but that's a part of life in many states. Even though I'd forced myself to go numb to all the things that had been happening around us, I realized that I'd begun to feel funny or different.

One morning, I woke and was hit by a panicked thought. I went directly into our bathroom and found a pregnancy test underneath my vanity. As I waited, I stared at the two little windows on the pregnancy test stick.

"Really, God? NOW?" I said aloud, as I shook my head.

A baby is always a blessing, and Matt and I couldn't have loved our two children more, but the timing seemed impossible. We had no health insurance and I had just started a new job, the first job I'd had since we lived in Sarasota. A month earlier, Matt and I had talked and we agreed that we needed to bring in more money if we were going to get ahead again. I'd gone to a local staffing agency in search of being placed with a company, but it turned out that the staffing company offered me a job to work there as a receptionist. I continued working, but I didn't share that I was pregnant.

When my manager at the staffing company eventually learned that I'd done so well with Mary Kay, I was offered a sales position within the staffing company. My new position with corporate would put me face-to-face with potential and existing business clients.

"You know I'm pregnant, right?" I said to my manager when she'd offered me the new position.

Her face told me she didn't have any clue, but we both knew she couldn't rescind the offer she'd just made. I knew, however, that she'd never regret hiring me, not for a minute.

Before long, my manager pulled me aside and said, "We'll be closing this location, but we've got a position for you in our Charlotte office."

I went home and talked about it with Matt. We'd only recently settled into our new home, but he supported me and he saw the potential for us.

"Okay! Let's do it!" he said.

Around this same time, one of Matt's customers had refused to pay him for an inspection, so he'd decided to get a job with TimeWarner that would provide a stable paycheck. Our relocation meant he'd have to do something else since it would be impossible for him to continue with TimeWarner.

Our little rental home in eastern Charlotte was cute, but since we were new to the area, we didn't realize we'd moved into a 'not too great' area. I quickly figured it out though and my suspicions were confirmed each time someone asked where I lived and then gasped when I replied, 'East Charlotte.'

My sales position with corporate had me traveling between Charlotte, Gastonia, and Kings Mountain. My pregnancy progressed as I simultaneously built a favorable reputation with the staffing company. I consistently met and exceeded my goals as I signed up clients and sold staffing services to companies. A great deal of travel made up my days as I pounded the pavement, continually in and out of offices and warehouses as I extolled the virtues of our company and vowed to consistently deliver stellar services. I wasn't just 'doing my job,' I really loved what I did, and maybe that's what was at the core of my success as my company increased my responsibilities when they saw that I could deliver.

Because I'd essentially 'opened our new branch,' I'd also worn many hats during the first five months in my new position. As I built my reputation in my job, Matt worked for himself and helped homeowners with loan modifications, something with which he was totally familiar. His knowledge of lending and banking made him the perfect person to help people in an area that's usually foreign to most.

· · ·

I took a little time off after I gave birth to our third child, but when I returned to work, I was offered a manager's position that would have me overseeing three geographic areas. The promotion allowed us to move to a more family-friendly, nicer area called Indian Trail. As I worked hard at my new position, Matt began to get into internet or 'digital' marketing while he simultaneously cared for our infant son while I was at work. In between baby feedings and diaper changes, Matt delved into the world of internet marketing.

Sometimes people are vague on what exactly 'internet marketing' is or does. In a nutshell, internet marketing generates customer interest in products and services using various strategies and techniques. Today it's a vital component in business development, branding, and sales for most companies and, for some businesses, internet marketing is the conduit to their customers and the lifeblood that keeps their companies afloat. Marketing is much broader and more complex than selling. It is often the ultimate, determining factor that turns people into buyers or customers. Therefore, it's a critical component that's at the core of many companies' sales strategies. Executed properly, internet marketing is the heartbeat that drives the success of many of today's most highly-regarded companies around the globe. Fortunately, it is also something in which Matt excels!

As the staffing company continued to grow, so did Matt's business. There was a time or two when I volunteered to personally stop and collect checks from some of his past-due clients. I may have arrived in neatly-pressed business clothes, but I was the dutiful Mama Bear that was on Matt's clients' doorsteps to collect what he was due. I didn't mind knocking on a stranger's front door and telling him 'I'd be happy to wait while he grabbed his checkbook.'

In time, a position came available in the staffing company's Safety Division. Although I didn't have the requisite education level that was required, I knew I could do the job, so I applied. Before long, I was hired as the company's Safety Manager. In my new role, I traveled North Carolina's east coast. I covered 800 to 1,000 miles a week as I made site visits to ensure that our clients complied with the safety standards set forth by our company.

Doing extremely well in my new position, I continued to swallow down all the hurt from our family's losses in Florida. I focused on my job, my husband, and our children, and I ignored the feelings that I ignored for so long. Matt worked from home, so he was the main caregiver for our children since my job had me on the road so much. The arrangement seemed to me like it was working, but other people had their own opinions.

"You're killing yourself!" my family repeatedly said.

"Your husband needs to take care of his family!" my brothers told me.

As I ignored my earlier pains and hurt, my family was constantly in my ear and feeding the gremlins that I'd tucked away. Even then, I knew they were just looking out for me. Their concerns came from a place of fear. They wanted to ensure my security and happiness. Sure, maybe I was sacrificing in some areas, but I was also rapidly climbing the corporate ladder and creating my own success. After I'd let go of my dreams with my own business, it felt good to have my hard work recognized and rewarded by the company for which I worked.

I reminded myself that 'with all successes also comes some sort of sacrifice.' It was this mantra that propelled me forth as I took on any work that needed to be done. No goal was too big, no objective too high. I'd do whatever necessary to get ahead. It's how I'm wired and probably how I got through some of our darkest days. Though I didn't think about it then, it's also part of the entrepreneurial mindset and what drives business owners to move forward, even when the chips are down. Back then though, I just took on any challenge and worked harder than anyone else as I chased my success!

After I'd proven myself in my role as our company Safety Manager, I was promoted to the position of Safety Director. With expanded responsibility also came an expanded geographic territory. My new position saw me covering the east coast of the US, from Florida all the way to Maine, and I now had Safety Managers that reported to me. With a much broader territory, I now flew between the states I covered.

As I gained traction in my new director's role, Matt gained traction with his internet marketing business too. Because we'd both worked so hard, we had dug our way out of debt, and so, we decided we wanted to purchase a home and once again become homeowners.

*"You never know how strong you are until being strong is all you have."*

*—unknown*

# 4
## STARTING OVER

FOR THE NEXT two years, we looked for a home that would suit our family's needs. Since he's got the mindset of an investor, Matt wanted to find a foreclosure, preferably a well-priced home in a good neighborhood, so we'd purchase some equity right away. I found a Craftsman style home in a neighborhood where all the houses sat nestled amongst a couple acres.

"I don't know," Matt said when I told him about the house I'd found.

"Come on, let's just go and have a look," I urged.

"Okay, God," Matt prayed, "If it's meant to be, then show me a hawk."

It should be noted that there are plenty of hawks in the area, so it wasn't as if he asked to see a unicorn as a sign that we should purchase the house. Asking for 'signs' was something that we'd done for quite some time. But in the past two years, as we'd searched for just the right home, Matt had also asked to see a hawk if we were meant to purchase any of the homes we'd toured.

For the next few days, we kept our eyes peeled for a hawk, the singular sign we'd asked to be given, but none appeared.

On the day that we'd planned to go and see the house, we talked about the fact that we hadn't yet seen the sign.

"Now, listen, Amy," Matt coached. "Don't let your excitement show when we're walking through the house. Play it close to your chest and try to keep your emotions in check, no matter how much you like it."

We both knew he was asking a lot. I'm a transparent personality in most cases and it's easy for others to read my reactions, but I knew Matt wanted to get the house for the best possible price if we both like it.

"I'll try," I promised.

We pulled up outside the newly built home that sat amongst two acres. Immediately, I envisioned our children playing on the lawn and riding their bikes throughout the family-oriented neighborhood. I was giddy with excitement as we got out of our car and met the realtor with whom we'd made an appointment to see the house. A huge grin was plastered across my face as I shook hands with the realtor. As we walked inside, Matt shot me a look to remind me to conceal my exuberance.

As we walked through the beautiful home, I imagined what it would be like to have our kids in it. I envisioned what it would be like to cook and serve dinner in the gorgeously-appointed kitchen and how cozy Matt and I would be as we curled up together in the family room. I felt like I'd bust at any moment, and I was careful not to look at the realtor's face, lest he read mine.

"I love it!" I finally burst. "I really love it!"

Matt just laughed, and the realtor looked pleased.

The home was beautiful, just what we'd both wanted, in fact. Matt is the kind of guy that looks at all scenarios, weighs the pros and cons, and then makes an informed decision about the next steps to take. For me, it was simple: I wanted to raise our family in that house. Matt knew how much I wanted the house. He walked through it again, room by room, and ended-up in the house's office that overlooked the backyard. Inch by inch, he painstakingly scanned the yard, the trees, and the shrubs for a hawk, the single sign we needed. Finally, I had to nearly drag Matt from the house.

"Come on! If it's meant to be, then it'll be," I said.

Just as we stepped over the door's threshold, Matt and I looked out at the tree opposite the house's front door. Right in front of us, plain as day, sat a beautiful hawk.

"Look!" Matt yelled as he pointed at the bird.

Matt and I looked at each other, and we both grinned as we continued to the car. My hands shook as I buckled my seatbelt and Matt started the car. The waterworks then began, and I felt flooded with emotion and happiness.

"Let's do it!" I smiled through my tears, as we held hands and drove out of our new neighborhood.

When we left, I couldn't contain my excitement, and it bubbled out, all at once. The house had seemed perfect! All the way home, Matt and I talked about it, how we'd enjoy it with our kids, and where we'd place the furniture.

"That was your best poker face?" he laughed. "Please don't ever go to Vegas or else we'll be broke."

To be honest, the house was a financial stretch for us. But my job was going well and Matt's business was growing. Plus, since some time had passed, our credit history looked more favorable than it had shortly after we'd left Florida. Purchasing the home would be a reach, but I really wanted to do it. Taking leaps of faith and taking on calculated risks is how an entrepreneur moves ahead, and it's always been the way we've lived our lives. Buying the home almost felt like a clean, fresh start for us, since life was going better by this time. It wouldn't be easy, but we'd make it work.

A few days later, and after we'd thought on it, Matt and I called the realtor and we submitted an offer, one of eight offers the seller had received. The seller verbally agreed to our terms, and we then went and signed the formal purchase contract. Afterward, we made a second appointment to walk through the house—our house. As we walked through it the second time, I was 'mentally arranging my furniture' in every room and I picked out rooms for each of the kids. An hour later, we shook hands with the realtor and told him we'd see him again at the closing. As we pulled away from our new home, I couldn't wait to decorate it for the holidays!

· · ·

Things were going well for us, and good things were just on the horizon as we looked forward to the closing on our new home. But I was still healing from everything that had happened in Florida. I didn't want to revisit all that pain and self-doubt. I preferred to focus on other things, so I didn't allow myself to feel the pain and devastation that I'd stuffed down and covered up for years. By now, I'd become a pro at suppressing my emotions. It was more of a habit than a survival technique by this point.

After our offer was accepted on the house, we then began the monumental task of providing all the financial documentation to the bank. Self-employed entrepreneurs know this is an arduous, seemingly endless chore. Working for oneself means having to provide mountains of documentation and proof of earnings that differ from what banks ask of typical employees that work for someone else. The whole undertaking is more complex and time-consuming for the nine million self-employed people in the US. Because business owners can legally take advantage of a slew of tax deductions, as related to their businesses, the result is a reduced taxable income. This is great for taxes, but it can present another hurdle when dealing with a lender. When mortgage underwriters review tax returns for proof of income, the figures represent the adjusted income after such deductions are made. Therefore, the impending result can reduce the amount of the loan for which the borrower may qualify. Some lenders are more familiar than others with dealing with self-employed borrowers and what this entails. In the end, we qualified for the loan to purchase our new home and we closed on it and moved our family into the home that had my heart from the moment I'd found it!

· · ·

After a while, I was headhunted by another company and I took a brief hiatus from the staffing company to go and pursue the Director's job that was offered to me. In the end though, I decided that I was happier with the staffing company that had initially taken a chance on this exuberant Florida girl with a 'can do' attitude. The staffing company eagerly rehired me as their Accounting Manager. They even sweetened the pot by allowing me to work from home in the new position that didn't require constant travel.

As I worked in my new capacity, Matt's business continued to grow and grow. He also began getting into network and affiliate marketing. Coincidentally, some of the best-known companies in the US, like Tupperware, Avon, and even Mary Kay, rely on the business model of network marketing. Affiliate marketing is a little more complex as it relies on the symbiotic relationship of four key players: the merchant (or retailer or brand), the network, the affiliate, and the customer. Affiliate marketing generally overlaps with other methods of internet marketing in some ways, since affiliates frequently utilize standardized practices like search engine optimization (SEO), pay per click (PPC), e-mail marketing, and display advertising. Today's merchants favor affiliate marketing because it's built on a 'pay for performance' business model, thereby making it a less costly marketing means.

Matt covered all the bases with his business and left no stone unturned. He went to symposiums, seminars, and conventions, and took advantage of any types of learning opportunities that he could use to grow his business. It was also advantageous for Matt to meet others in the industry and have people to talk with that understood the business and the challenges he faced.

With today's fast-paced economic climate, coupled with customers' demands for immediate gratification, Matt must constantly stay current with all facets of his industry, along with what's happening in the world. This led to Matt's realization that others could benefit from his experience, so he also began to do coaching. In time, Matt melded together his marketing expertise, his hands-on experience as an entrepreneur, and his love of people and he became a consultant and speaker. Like most successful entrepreneurs, he realized the importance of not only having mentors but of also being a mentor and giving back.

Matt was enriching himself, expanding his horizons, and challenging himself to grow, not only in his business but also as a person. I was on the sidelines as I watched my husband's self-growth, and while I was proud of Matt, I began to realize that I was unfulfilled. There was something missing, but I just couldn't pinpoint what it was that I needed in my life. It was as if a little piece of me were missing, and since I couldn't identify it, I couldn't go out and get it for myself. Although my job was great, Matt's business was doing well, we were blessed with amazing kids, and we had a wonderful home, I was constantly nagged by the feeling that I was supposed to be doing something else. I went along like this for a while, simply existing, but not really living. It was a difficult and miserable time for me, even though to most people, it looked like I had it all.

As 2014 progressed, I became more and more unsettled, and I grew resentful—but at what? I couldn't put my finger on the source of my feelings. I'd begun hanging around a low-energy group of people that lacked aspirations and solid goals. To them, the future wasn't any further than 'tomorrow,' and they were short-sighted and without dreams or purpose.

Matt traveled all the time that year. I missed him when he was gone, but my new group of friends did little to make me feel better while he was away.

"If he's gone all the time, then you must be the last thing on his mind," they'd scoff. "If he cared about his wife, then he'd be at home with her. Money isn't everything!"

Their comments only fueled my insecurities. My mind conjured up various scenarios that did nothing good for how I was feeling.

Matt went to various events, did speaking gigs, networked, and constantly learned about niches, e-commerce, and advancements within his industry. In his line of work, it is critical that he stay current on trends and advancements. He traveled with a good friend of his, but to me, it seemed like he was 'with his tribe' and I was not a member of that special tribe that had so much in common with him. I was an outsider and not a part of the life Matt had apart from our marriage. Sure, we shared a bed, children, and a home, but in my mind, Matt had his 'home life' and 'his business life' and I was not a part of the latter.

The fact that my husband spent $50,000 on travel expenses that year only added fuel to the already smoldering fire within me. I'd been pushing down my angst for so long, and my internal feelings of self-doubt seethed just beneath the surface. I didn't recognize it at the time, but a 'perfect storm' was brewing and gaining strength, just waiting to explode and rain down on us and our marriage.

Matt didn't understand what was happening inside of me. All he saw was a wife that didn't believe in him and the future that he envisioned. He probably felt alone too, and he sought support from 'his tribe' as I wrestled with my internal anguish and doubts, unaware of what was happening with myself. I didn't feel like I was a part of Matt's dream, as if he pushed forth on his own as I stood alone on the side of the road as he pressed on toward his goals. The divide between us continued to grow wider and we grew apart. While I'd once been enamored and inspired by Matt's enthusiasm and zest for success, I didn't feel that I was 'with him on the ride' anymore.

Since I felt alone, I hung out with my own set of people, as Matt kept busy with his tribe and his plans. Unfortunately, because I was vulnerable and impressionable in my weakened state, I allowed myself to be around some negative, toxic people. Their comments and opinions were overwhelming and infectious, and I allowed myself to be infected by them.

"Well, if he's off on all these trips, how do you know what he's up to?" they'd ask.

"Yeah, I've heard what goes on at conventions! When the cat's away, the mice will play!" some said.

"Men always look! And some women will leap on successful men and attach themselves, whether the men are married or not!"

Since I wasn't talking to or interacting with my husband, it was easy for my head to be filled with the wrong sort of damaging innuendo. The negativity infected me and spread like a poison. The monster within gained power and rose steadily toward the surface, like a rattling covered pot steadily coming to a rolling boil, the heat just beginning to break the surface with more and more force that threatened to blow the top off.

When Matt and I did speak, our exchanges were usually ugly and hurtful, designed to damage and cut. Years earlier, I could have never imagined that Matt and I could be so hateful and venomous toward one another. I've heard it said that when there's passion in a marriage, it comes out in both the good times and the bad. We had loved passionately, and so we fought with the same unbridled intensity, cutting deep and going for the jugular. Every day we hurt each other with our words and our actions. Looking back, even I am shocked by the ugly, hateful diatribe that spewed freely from me and onto the person I love most in the world. It's a time that I wish we could forever erase from our memories and, even today, I still haven't forgiven myself for my behavior.

The venomous toxicity threatened to overtake and forever damage the marriage I had treasured above all else. Our hateful exchanges wreaked havoc and imperiled the union that we'd once held dear. Matt and I had once promised to 'love, honor, and protect,' but in the moment, those vows seemed so long ago and like hushed whispers, just faintly noticeable beneath the gale force winds that ominously warned of what was headed toward us. My feelings of uncertainty and self-doubt took over completely and spun me like an out-of-control fair ride. I was a hapless passenger, being flung about, to and from, as the ride picked up speed. The intensity grew and grew until I finally erupted.

"That's IT! I'm leaving!" I proclaimed, at the end of 2014.

My declaration was the result of desperate frustration. I was at my wit's end, confused, overwhelmed, and hopeless. All the negativity that I'd heard had pooled inside me, alternately churning and rising as it fed my insecurities and stress. The ugly monster had taken on a life of its own, and it only grew more powerful in the wake of the negative chatter and tenuous times. It wasn't obvious at the time, but I'd later be able to look back with a clear head and a fresh perspective, and I would recognize what had been happening.

Every married person, no matter how long they've been together, deals with similar angst at some point, so I know most people can understand my plight. In the moment though, it felt like Matt and I simply couldn't relate and connect. I resented that he 'wasn't hearing me' and Matt felt that I was becoming someone he didn't even recognize anymore.

I'm not really a 'drinker' by any stretch of the imagination and yet, I sought comfort in a glass of wine. That 'glass' soon became a bottle and I regularly drank each night—to the point of passing out. It seemed like my only escape and the only way to numb the pain and chaos inside myself. We'd stopped going to church, and I became reclusive, preferring to stay alone in the dark rather than be burdened with dealing with people. I didn't have the energy, nor the inclination, to be bothered—with anything or anyone.

In time, I allowed a few select people into my dark world, but I chose the wrong ones to trust and take into my confidence. In the moment, it seemed like they had my best interest at heart, but they did not, not at all. They acted concerned, under the guise of helping me, but allowing them into my pain was like pouring gasoline onto a fire. Their negativity only fueled the monster that swelled within me as I built a fortress around myself that not even Matt could permeate. His words and actions couldn't reach me. In time, his cries and pleas turned to anger and he stopped caring whether I was involved in what he was building.

Choosing to flee my negative, tormented soul, Matt preferred to attend more events that put him around positive people with happy outlooks on life. He thrived in an environment of entrepreneurs that shared his positivity and 'can do' spirit, and he certainly wasn't getting those affirmations from his wife. In time, I'd realize that such events were Matt's only means of escape and, quite possibly, his way of maintaining his sanity as his wife slipped further and further away.

For centuries, it's been no secret that women are more emotional beings, and that's what makes us nurturers. From a physiological standpoint, women have four times as many brain cells as men, something that's scientifically measurable. Well, all my cells were on high-alert and firing on all cylinders as I wrestled the gremlins that chattered about how I deserved better and how I should 'find myself' and 'reach my potential.' Men use their left brain to problem-solve, while we use both sides, but sometimes, all that traffic and activity becomes a lot to handle. Coupled with our emotions and hormones, it can create a firestorm. Research even shows that women can process and transfer data between the right- and left-brain hemispheres faster than men. Some might say this puts men at a slight disadvantage at times. While our brains are eight percent smaller than men's brains, we have more interconnections that lead to more finite situational thinking.

Men, on the other hand, are spatial thinkers that revert to pattern prediction when faced with problems. The fact that women's brains allow us to multi-task, while men must perform individual tasks one at a time, may also put men at a disadvantage at times. Our larger limbic system makes us more expressive (ahem!) than our male counterparts too, but men sometimes have a difficult time understanding our expressions and rapid-fire delivery of what we're thinking and feeling.

What's all this mean? In a nutshell, Matt realized his wife felt under-appreciated, unfulfilled and in need of enrichment in her search for her purpose! Of course, at the end of 2014, I wasn't thinking about science and the differences in men and women. All I knew was that I was miserable and that something had to change.

Even today, I'm careful to speak only from my side of things and my perspective. I know Matt has his own take on how things unfolded in our life, but I can only share my experience of how things occurred to the best of my recollection. It's easy to place blame to justify one's actions or reactions, but that's not the same as taking responsibility.

When we separated, our kids were fourteen, nine, and six years old. Matt didn't want the separation, and yet, at the same time, he probably felt somewhat relieved for the distance it put between us, so we could gain better perspectives on things. There had been so much anger between us that the environment had grown toxic and unproductive. I saw no other option at the time and I felt hopeless, lost, and confused. It was still hard on the kids, and both Matt and I hated that part of it.

*"Above all else guard your heat, for everything you do flows from it."*

*Proverbs 4:23*

# 5

# FINDING PERSPECTIVE

MATT AND I LIVED separately, with him at our family home and the kids and I at a nearby rented bungalow. There was so much hurt, anger, and resentment between us that it no longer seemed like we could reach one another, even if we tried. In recent months, it had felt as if our marriage had taken on a life of its own and like Matt and I had been strangers. Neither one of us recognized the other, much less the person we'd each become.

I knew that if I'd stayed in the house with Matt that no good would have come of it. There was just too much contempt and ugliness at the time. He and I were both too close to the situation, and we were each reeling from our own pains and bitter feelings. It wasn't healthy and there was no way we could have productively communicated at the time.

Prior to the last year, I'd had a close connection to God. But as things began to unravel, I allowed myself to drift away and disconnect from Him. I'd previously gone to church with Matt, and we had both grown close to our pastor. I had no explanation for why I'd pulled back from God and the church, especially at a time when I needed both.

I can't say that I was happy in our new living arrangement, but it did allow me to think and try to gain a new perspective on things. After about three months, I began to see things from a different vantage point. The time and space had allowed me to admit to myself that I'd been operating from a place of hurt. I realized that nothing positive could come out of the pain if I didn't deal with it.

One morning, I woke and quietly lingered in bed, just thinking about how things had spiraled out of control over the last year. I hated how I'd been feeling, and I didn't like the person that stared back at me from the mirror each day. All at once, the tears began to pour from me as if someone had turned on a faucet. Sobs wracked my body as I pulled the covers up to my neck and cried. I thought about Matt's recent call and how he'd asked to see me. He'd tried to convince me that I should come back, but I just wasn't ready. I was so confused.

Hours later, I got a phone call and was surprised to hear my pastor's voice. "I'm on your side of town, Amy," he said. "Can I stop by and see you?"

His comment was odd because the church wasn't nearby, and I didn't think he really had business in my area. But hearing his voice had somehow softened my heart, and I told him to come by the house.

Although I didn't realize it at the time, what came next would be a pivotal moment and a turning point in my life and in my marriage. There are no accidents, and it was no accident that my pastor came by to talk to me on that day when I was so lost, just hours after I'd started my day in tears, feeling defeated and confused.

As I talked with my pastor, I realized that God had stepped in to help me and that He'd sent help, in the form of my pastor, a man who was like a father figure as he delivered his words of advice. His visit that day was a turning point for me and just what I needed at that moment.

"So, we'll see you on Sunday?" the pastor asked, as he said goodbye that afternoon.

"I'll be there," I smiled.

On Super Bowl Sunday, the kids and I went to church. After the service had ended, the pastor asked me and Matt to stay and talk with him.

"Amy and Matt, you both need to stop all this, and you need to get your life together again," he told us.

It was as if God had stepped in and said, "That's enough, children." His divine intervention and the pastor's counsel were just what we needed to find clarity and get a handle on things. It helped us to get control of our runaway marriage that had been running amok and taking us off-course.

As we left the pastor, Matt said, "Hey, do you want to hang out tonight?"

"Sure, you can come over, and we can watch the Super Bowl," I said.

When Matt came over later, the kids were over at their friends' houses, so we could be alone and talk. We talked and cried, uninterrupted for hours. It was just what we both had needed for so long. I think we each heard the other, really heard the other, and thought about each other's perspectives on things. From that night on, Matt and I were never again apart.

I wasn't ready to move back into our family home just yet though. It was the place that had held some bad feelings and negative energy from the past year. So, Matt moved into our little bungalow as he and I worked on our marriage. It was probably good for us to be in a place other than our main home while we worked on things.

After a couple of months, we decided that living with our family in a 1400-square-foot home, when we had a nice 3600-square-foot home, just didn't make the best sense, so we took the kids and moved back to our main home. As crazy as it sounds, the separation had been good for us, since it made us realize what we had in the other, in our family, and in our marriage. It gave us a broader perspective and made us look at our own mistakes. It gave us a deeper clarity and let us reevaluate what we wanted in life, in our family, and in our marriage.

I realized that I had to engage and become a participatory player in Matt's world. This was reinforced though when I attended one of his events and started meeting and talking with the other attendees. I immediately noticed that there were hardly any women at the first event.

"Where are all the women, the wives, and the girlfriends?" I asked one man.

"Oh, you've got to talk to my wife! She feels just like you do—that there aren't enough women at these things," he laughed.

Later that night, as we drove home from the event, Matt and I talked about it and about the people I'd met there.

"You know," I said, "It's different for the entrepreneurial wives. The things we deal with, our perspectives, and our feelings are so different from yours and from husbands' in general."

Matt understood what I was talking about and he agreed that wives, and women have entirely different roles in the entrepreneurial marriage. Because being an entrepreneur encompasses all areas of a business owner's life, his wife is also affected by his work, his dreams, his stresses, and his successes. Entrepreneurship isn't a nine-to-five job; it's a lifestyle, and one that includes the spouses and the families. This is where the concept of The Entrepreneur's Wife project began.

• • •

Sometime later, after I'd attended Matt's event, we went to a small event by Sean Stephenson, an American therapist, self-help author, and motivational speaker. Born with osteogenesis imperfecta, Stephenson uses a wheelchair, has fragile bones, and stands three feet tall, but he motivated the crowd as if he were a giant. Stephenson began giving speeches at the age of seventeen, and it was easy to see why the audience basked in his inspirational message. He explained how people could develop a 'stuck energy' that makes us lash out and react in negative ways to get the stuck energy to move and leave us. This lashing out can be through yelling, drinking, drugs, or other self-destructive behaviors.

It felt as if our speaker was speaking only to me, like he'd known of my earlier journey and the obstacles I'd faced. It was truly an 'Aha Moment' and one I'll never forget. I realized that I'd developed my own 'stuck energy' and that I had gone down a path of decisions and behaviors that could have destroyed the very marriage that I treasured more than anything. As I listened to Stephenson, I knew I'd found the final inspiration that I needed to take the next step on my journey. The Entrepreneur's Wife would be the perfect way to connect with women like myself who needed to know how to navigate their roles in life, and I'd use my own firsthand experience as the catalyst to bring together the women.

Wanting to find resources for entrepreneurial wives, I went to my computer and searched for resources that spoke to our specific needs and interests. There were a few sites that dealt specifically with 'military wives' and their unique issues, but there was nothing geared to 'entrepreneurial wives.' I was even more positive that I could BE the resource for women. Like all entrepreneurs, I 'found a need and filled it.'

We all learn from those that went before us, and that's the idea behind The Entrepreneur's Wife. While no two entrepreneurial marriages are the same, they all share many commonalities. Sometimes just knowing that others have 'walked the walk' is all women need, but we strive to provide everything from a sounding board to suggestions on how to deal with the very finite and specific issues that affect entrepreneurial relationships. Just as entrepreneurship is a continuous journey, so is being an entrepreneur's wife. We take the ride alongside our husbands, sometimes as their companion, their cheerleader, their confidante, their soft place to land, and their rock during difficult times. We share their stresses and their successes along the journey.

When I first started The Entrepreneur's Wife, I needed to learn more about the women and their viewpoints. This led me to connect with the ladies that shared the same mindset as I do. I started a Facebook page and Blog where I told my own story. People immediately reached out, grateful that someone else related to their own journeys and unique circumstances. Both women and men were pleased to find a place where they felt they 'fit in' and could 'be heard.' People wrote letters and sent messages of their own trials as they made their way through their journeys. I soon realized that I'd gone through the last years so that I could relate to others and make a difference in their lives and the level of fulfillment they found in their entrepreneurial marriages. There are no accidents. God knew that I had to fall and then rebuild myself and our marriage so that I could identify with others and help them through their issues and over their hurdles. If I'd never gone through my own hard times, I'd never be able to relate to them.

Although I'd found my purpose, I still leaned on God. I prayed often and went to Him with my questions and asked for His guidance. In addition to being closer to God again, I also decided to take a long, hard look at all the people in my life. We're all affected by those people in our Circle of Influence, so I decided to be more particular about who I let into my circle. There was no value in allowing toxic, negative voices into my marriage, especially since Matt and I had begun healing and we'd started to grow again as a couple.

I prayed, "God, please only allow people into our lives that'll help us and not hurt us."

My friend groups had changed. I'd let go of some relationships that I didn't find healthy or positive and I chose to only associate with people who shared my same values, ideals, and morals. It was my way of protecting and safeguarding the marriage that meant so much to me. In all things, I put my marriage first, since it's the foundation on which we'd built our family and it's the thing at the nucleus of all we hold dear.

The overall divorce rate in America lingers around fifty percent, yet for entrepreneurial couples, the divorce rate is seventy percent. It's easy to see how it's higher amongst entrepreneurial couples than those in the general population, who have jobs and employers. There may be many reasons for this, and admittedly, all marriages have their own unique, intimate issues, but one thing is for certain: A business can swallow a marriage whole before either party knows what happened! Being an entrepreneur is a lifestyle, so therefore it becomes all-consuming. But just as a business requires work, so does a marriage. Just as clients and accounts must be tended, so does a marriage. Just as business owners meet with employees and discuss issues and goals, so should husbands and wives meet regularly and communicate about their visions and dreams.

A business can be seen by wives as 'an affair,' a distraction that takes their husbands' time, energy, and focus from them and their families. The wife may resent it when her entrepreneur husband is passionate and fired up with excitement and anticipation as his business grows. The business takes on a life of its own and can easily become 'the other woman' that takes up a husband's whole focus. The husband, however, doesn't see it like this. He has the pressure of making sure the business succeeds so he can take care of his family and their needs. He is innately wired to be 'the hunter,' the one charged with providing the sustenance for his family. When wives realize this, they begin to understand that the business is not the enemy, but that it's the vehicle that they can both take toward their joint goals in life. In life, sometimes we're the leaders, and sometimes we are the followers. Sometimes we're the drivers, sometimes the passengers. In marriage, we share those same roles too, but even when wives are the passengers, they can help navigate during the journey and make their own contributions that help lead them to their destinations.

After we got back together, I asked Matt's forgiveness for hurting him when I'd lost my way. He told me that I needed to also forgive myself, but I wasn't ready quite yet to do that. As Matt and I began to mend our marriage, our hearts started to heal too, and we felt closer and stronger than before. We'd weathered another storm and had come out of it—together. Sometimes we must be brought to our lowest point to be put on the path that we were meant to walk. We look up when we are on our knees, desperate and pleading to find direction and strength. But without the struggle, we'd never find our strength, and there's power in that strength. As Darla Evans once said, "*Those scars you accumulated are the markings of a warrior*" and I wear mine with pride.

# BUILDING THE FOUNDATION

# 6

# ISN'T MARRIAGE FOREVER?

IT'S A SAD reality that today's society so casually accepts as a social norm that marriage is not forever. Why even enter into a marriage with the expectation that it won't last? Entrepreneurs wouldn't dream of giving up on their business, their baby, the lifeblood of their existence. So then, why isn't it always their first instinct to fight as hard for their marriage when it hits a rocky patch?

We have let ourselves believe that failing in our relationship has no effect on our business. I do not believe this to be so. For entrepreneurs, their identity as a business owner isn't something that's turned off and on. It is an integral part of their being. It affects every aspect of their life, including their relationships. It's in an entrepreneur's makeup to hustle and grind for the success of their business, so the same amount of effort should also go into their marriage. Sure, it's easy to ignore things, look the other way, and hope issues will disappear. But they usually don't. In fact, they usually gain strength, grow, and sometimes take on a menacing life of their own. It's possible to hide from the truth for a while, but eventually, it comes out. It might peek out, little by little, or it might all at once kick down the door and consume everyone in its path, leaving a trail of destruction in its wake. Either way, rest assured that when issues are left untended and unaddressed, they do not just go away.

Most entrepreneurs have goals, and they create action plans to take them to those goals. They use different metrics by which they measure their progress, and when necessary, they adjust their tactics and change their strategy at times. The same ideals and methods can be applied in one's personal life too. If you're not getting what you need in your home or personal life, then it is your responsibility to analyze the situation and identify the issues. Once you've figured out what you want or need, there are various ways to obtain it.

Just as entrepreneurs use marketing plans, we can also employ similar theory to our marriages and our relationships. A comprehensive marketing strategy is the foundation of a great marketing plan, just as the love that first brought together a couple is also the foundation of their marriage. In business, when times get tough, many entrepreneurs choose to 'get back to basics' and get a handle on their business so they can once again steer it and guide it. This is exactly what's needed when couples feel they're pulling away from one another or going down different paths.

Most entrepreneurs will do anything and everything to salvage a client, or on a larger scale, to salvage their business. It's the same with marriage. All that's needed is a plan, commitment, and the tools to affect change and obtain the desired results. If sales numbers are low, business owners look at many factors, like the effectiveness of their sales personnel, their products or services, current market conditions, their competition, and other factors that may be the cause of lower figures. One by one, each factor is evaluated. If the business owner finds his company is lacking in any area, he then adjusts his strategy. He may hire coaches for his team or invest more money in packaging or branding so his wares stand out in the market. He'll then set a timeframe in which to measure the progress of his implemented changes, and he will chart and track the results to gauge whether his realigned methods have been successful.

When his sales figures are plummeting, or his client list is dwindling, an entrepreneur won't stand idly by and watch his empire crumble around his feet. He'll invest research, time, money, energy, and whatever it takes to turn things around and salvage his business. The same proactive mindset works where relationships or marriages are concerned. When a business is left untended, it will eventually die off, and so will a marriage.

Being selfish is just as important as being selfless when a marriage is at stake. Sometimes it's tough to be either. But if we treat our marriage with the same enthusiasm, dedication, curiosity, belief, and non-stop hustle that we use in our business, then our relationship will be unstoppable too. We brag about being different, being an entrepreneur, and thinking outside of the box. We'd never give up on our dreams of entrepreneurial success, and we want to shout from the mountaintops about our businesses. Similarly, I think there should be more bragging about having a happy marriage.

Loving our work is a gift but loving our work also can make it easy to neglect other parts of our life. As an entrepreneur, we decide where our time goes. We decide how to prioritize all areas of our lives. We steer our lives and the paths we'll take along our journey. Just like in entrepreneurship, 'the buck stops here,' with us when it comes to our relationships and marriages.

It felt good to be back on track, alongside Matt, and jointly working toward strengthening our marriage. Many of the changes we'd made, like being around like-minded people who shared our values and life goals, was key to beginning to renew and safeguard our marriage. Once again, we were 'rowing in the same direction' and moving toward our joint goals. Putting our marriage first allowed all the other facets of our lives to align too and fall into place. There was a tactile, tangible shift that was felt by both of us.

This is not to say that our marriage was, or ever would be, entirely perfect. It meant though that we were stronger and better able to handle situations when they arose. If Matt and I had to make decisions, we first asked ourselves 'What best serves our common goals?' Even if we didn't always agree on all things, there was one thing on which we did agree: that our marriage was the foundation for the rest of our world. It felt good to have realigned our priorities and to work toward the same things that would reinforce our commitment to one another and to our family.

• • •

At the beginning of 2016, I decided to resign from my job and to focus on other things. Today Matt and I run a fitness apparel company and a dietary supplement company. Matt still runs his internet marketing company and he also owns a software start-up called Ecomisoft that builds apps for virtual storefront owners. Branded as The Lifestyle Architect, Matt shares his methods and metrics of how others can design and create the life they desire while I run my business, The Entrepreneur's Wife. Although we've been through some very difficult and trying times, we know that they were necessary for us to help and guide others.

The takeaway from 'the dark period' in our marriage is invaluable today, not just to us, but also to others. We know what it's like to be the entrepreneur and what's it's like to be married to the entrepreneur. My observations and experiences have given me insights that I share with others. I was lonely and felt virtually all alone as I dealt with the issues that affected my marriage and myself. With my help, it's my hope that other women won't have to experience those unproductive, hurtful feelings and detrimental situations.

Once the entrepreneur and his spouse discuss their goals, it's then important to identify the roles each will play in pursuit of those common goals. This solidifies that both are integral and important parts of the process. Two are stronger than one, and there are benefits to working together as a team, both in the business and within the marriage.

Discuss expectations of each part of the team and how he or she will function in the business and the marriage and family. This makes sure both sides are heard and leaves no room for gray areas that can later lead to resentment and hurt feelings. Plus, it opens the lines of communications on a deeper level. Since entrepreneurs steer their businesses, they may feel they must also steer their home life or they may prefer to leave that to their spouse and make it entirely her domain. It's important to talk about how such dynamics will work within the marriage and to give clarity of expectations in these areas. Never assume that your spouse wants or expects anything! Ask, discuss, share, and communicate on all issues of your lives!

Just like in business, entrepreneurs have goals, both long-term and short-term, and they measure their progress along the way. Within the marriage, when milestones or goals are met, it's important to slow down and celebrate them, no matter how big or small, as a team. This reinforces the roles and importance of both people within the marriage.

Talk about your family's overall mission and the way you'd like for your family to be viewed by the outside world. Businesses have mission statements, or statements of purpose, around which all activities of the company are based. Every employee, from top to lower-level, must adhere to and reinforce the statements of their company and uphold its tenets in all they do. These mission statements expressly identify the core values that are important to the company and how they will be upheld. It's the same with a family. Agree on your family's and your marriage's overall philosophy and how all members of the family can do their part to uphold it.

Just like companies employ branding strategy to gain the trust, respect, and recognition needed to thrive, so can families. Consider how you'd like for your family and its members to be viewed. Talk about what each member can do to 'reinforce your brand.' This is especially important when children are involved. It 'makes them a part of the team' and 'reinforces the values of their parents,' which allows them to make the best decisions that will uphold 'the brand' and 'reflect well on the family.'

As companies utilize business plans to plot their goals and support their mission statements, families and marriages can also do the same. Sometimes business plans may be altered, edited, or scrapped altogether, in favor of new or better ones. It's fine to do this within personal relationships too. Circumstances change, people grow, goals are affected, and the wants and needs of people differ over time.

It's perfectly acceptable to edit or change the business plan that spells from time to time. The biggest, and most important, component though is the 'people' within the family or marriage. A business is only as good as its people, just as a family or marriage is only as good as its people! Similarly, people are a company's biggest asset, just as people are the biggest assets of a family or a marriage!

Consider what you want your family or marriage to represent, how those ideas will be presented and upheld, and how each person can do his or her part to ensure the unit runs efficiently so everyone profits from the relationships. Like a business, a husband and wife come together to form a merger that will benefit both, and they feel they'll be better, stronger, and more successful if they are together. The conglomerate of people within a marriage or a family bring with them their own special and unique talents and attributes that can strengthen the brand and market it to others. The greatest satisfaction comes years later, when the husband and wife watch as their own kids 'franchise' their parents' 'company' and build their own families, modeled after the ones in which they were raised! THAT's when you know you've found success!

*"It's not the lack of love, but the lack of friendship that makes unhappy marriages."*

—*Friedrich Nietzsche*

# 1
# COMMUNICATION IS KEY

COMMUNICATION IS KEY to so many things in life. Relationships of all kinds benefit, grow, and thrive thanks to communication. But communicating, by definition, is 'the exchanging of information or news.' Styles of communication differ, but the most important thing to remember is to 'listen,' not only talk. Everyone is different, and we all come from unique backgrounds and circumstances. These things affect how we share and receive information. It's important to find what works for you and your partner and to agree on how you will communicate.

In addition to communicating, it is vital to know how our spouse communicates. This information ensures we can 'speak so that he hears us.' Since people collect and assimilate details and data differently, take the time to decipher how your spouse intakes and outputs conversation. There's no right or wrong way to receive conversation, so be flexible if your mate's methods differ from your own. We're all products of our upbringings, our environments, and our unique experiences, and these may vastly differ. Take these things into account and figure out how your spouse receives communication from you. The following questions may help determine how your spouse communicates and receives communication:

*Is your spouse analytical?*

*Is he overtly expressive?*

*Is he emotionally stagnated?*

*Was he raised in a home where one parent was dominant?*

*Is he a liberal free-thinker?*

*Is he judgmental toward others?*

*Does he withhold his opinions and emotions?*

*Does he feel that he must explain himself?*

*Does he often feel defensive?*

*Does he have to always control a conversation?*

*Does he look for cues from you as to how to react or are his responses genuine?*

*Does he trust you with his feelings?*

*Does he feel judged?*

Styles of communication, and understanding how a spouse processes communication, can completely affect a situation, for better or for worse. Sometimes the simplest of things can get blown out of proportion, or important issues may not be given enough credence.

Take the time to discuss communication styles with your partner and agree on how you'll relate in the future. When the need arises for you to talk with your partner, or anyone else for that matter, know when to start the conversation. If your spouse is running late, trying to get out the door, and searching for his car keys, it's probably not the best time to talk about anything meaningful.

• • •

In our case, there was a time when I felt like Matt worked twenty hours a day, and when he was physically with me, it felt like he wasn't completely engaged and attuned to what was going on. I realize now that he was so immersed in his business because he had to make it work, had to make it a success. His family's lifestyle and very survival depended on it! As the man, he was the hunter that brought home sustenance for his family. In his mind, it was his ultimate responsibility. Matt was just doing what he thought he was supposed to do. But at the time, all I felt was unimportant and insubstantial. It felt to me that Matt's work and his business were more important than me.

I grew to hate his cell phone. It was like a constant wedge between us, and when it rang, it took my husband even further away. Even when I tried to talk to him about something, I knew that if his phone rang, I'd have to pause and wait for him to finish dealing with a client or business partner. It seemed like he was disinterested in my conversation and as if I were an imposition on his time. In those days, I didn't see Matt's phone as the conduit to our family's financial success. It was instead simply an intruder that I came to hate. Over time, and once Matt and I had reconciled, I felt more like we were on the same team, and I regarded the phone interruptions as a necessary part of an entrepreneur's life since it's not the typical nine-to-five scenario. In addition, Matt has gotten better about being engaged and present when we talk. He's also learned to fight the urge to check his phone for emails and texts quite as often as he once did. Today, when I need to talk to him about something, I first pick the best time to have the conversation. Matt appreciates the consideration, and when we talk, he gives me his attention because he realizes this.

...

After you've picked the best time to talk, consider how you'll share information and how your partner will receive it. Remember, it is a conversation, not a one-sided information or opinion delivery. For instance, talking at someone is not communicating at all. It's a one-sided monolog intended to barrage the listener with one's own opinions and feelings. Invite comments, ideas, opinions, and sharing from your partner. The exchange makes both people feel invested in the topic at hand and allows for both voices to be heard.

Always be respectful. Consider how you'd talk to a colleague or a friend and approach your partner with the same respect. Never resort to name-calling or dredging-up 'old history' that's not relevant to the conversation. Comments of 'You're such a jerk!' or 'Why did I marry someone that's so stupid?' are not things you really want to say, and they're hurtful daggers that can't be taken back. Such attacks serve no purpose, and they only divert attention from the real issue at hand. They're unproductive, lead to resentment, and stall, if not stop, the progress of communication. Use a calm tone and avoid anger and finger-pointing. Abstain from phrases that begin with 'I hate it when you...' or 'You always...'. They circumvent the real topic of discussion, and they lead to nothing but defensiveness in your partner. No resolution ever comes from sentences that start out like this.

Look at it like this: Would you attack a colleague, an employee, or a client with hurtful verbal assaults? If you did, what would they think of you? Would you still have credibility with those people if you resorted to aggressive attacks? Of course not! They'd regard you as an unprofessional, petulant child and they'd lose respect for you! It's easy to be so comfortable with our spouse that our 'lips become a little looser' at times, but in the end, fight the urge to spout off with ugly remarks that serve no purpose.

It's important to be heard, and it's only natural to want to stand our ground and defend our positions and viewpoints. Knowing how and when to make ourselves heard puts us one step closer to getting what we want out of a situation. Our 'delivery' is the next critical component in arguing our position in an argument. In the end, talking things out is best for all concerned. Making known our feelings also unburdens us and lets us feel more mentally healthy, which leads to better overall health and a happier home for everyone in it.

Bottling up feelings only works for so long, and when the lid finally blows, the results can be catastrophic for whoever is in the 'danger zone' to receive the fallout. Avoidance of a conversation is never a good thing. An issue can be postponed to a later time that's more suitable and when you feel ready to have the conversation but pushing things down and not talking about them never ends well. If you understand how your partner 'hears you,' then you'll know how to best talk to him, and this includes arguing with him too. An argument need not become a heated, hate-filled, eruptive episode. In fact, such an exchange is only non-productive and usually doesn't lead to resolution or satisfaction for either party. But, let's be honest. We've all been there, at least a time or two, and have said things we wish we could take back. It's human nature to be passionate about things that matter to us, but if we turn that passion into a productive exchange, an argument can merely be an exchange in which we present and defend our stance on an issue.

An example of this is when lawyers 'argue' cases in court. They rationally present their assertions and back up their commentary. That's exactly what we can do too when we 'argue' with our partners or spouses. The main thing to remember is to only fight with a purpose. Wanton, reckless arguing serves no purpose and only inflicts harm on the other person and the marriage. Even if your opposing views may be violently conflicted, the argument need not escalate to something reminiscent of a World War. Remember, you love your partner, he's not your opponent.

There are techniques for how to have a productive argument. First, agree that you'll remain calm and that neither you nor your partner will resort to hitting below the belt, dredging up old contentious issues or name-calling. Make your goal to explain your issue, your opinions on it, and how it affects you, your marriage, or your family. Insist your partner hears you out entirely without interjecting and then allow him to explain his stance while you remain quiet (Remember, negative body language, eye-rolling, and heavy sighs will only add fuel to the fire.). After he's explained his standpoint on the issue, ask questions if you require clarification or further explanation. And finally, try to find a compromise that allows you to both 'meet in the middle,' each giving just a little for the sake of your union.

No matter how long we've known our partners, there's always something new to learn and discover. That's what keeps it interesting! One thing that's important to find out is what 'love expression' your partner prefers. What's the one thing that makes him know he is truly loved by you? People generally prefer to give love in the ways that they like to receive it, but that won't work if their partner identifies with a different love language. Find out what makes your partner feel loved. Does he like to spend time together? Does he feel especially loved when you do things for him, like pick up his dry cleaning or bake his favorite cake? Is it important to him that he hears words of affirmation? Does he enjoy receiving tokens of affection that let him know you were thinking of him? Is physical touch, or even sex, the thing that makes him feel most loved? The biggest and most important thing we can communicate to our partner is that they are loved. Take the time to find out what makes him feel loved and express love in the way that he best understands.

In addition to knowing how our partner prefers to receive love, we also must discern what triggers him to feel angry, defensive, or defeated. When we know what these triggers are, we also know how to avoid them, since they're unproductive and sometimes destructive.

We must also know our own triggers, so we can spot them, take control, and avoid taking our own next step to anger or negative responses. A trigger is something that sets off a memory tape or a flashback that transports you back to the event of your original trauma with a person. We all have emotional triggers. You know the feeling when someone makes a comment that might not be a huge deal to another person, but it totally throws you off balance for the rest of the day? That's your trigger.

When faced with our personal triggers, it's usually not what IT is that makes us uncomfortable. It's how IT makes us feel, and our brain accepts the trigger as a stimulus to react.

Our mind recalls how we felt the last time we dealt with the trigger, and our emotions repeat those same feelings and reactions. Everyone has different triggers, but here are a few common ones and the reactions they evoke:

✓ Someone rejecting you, as if you're not good enough

✓ Someone abandoning you (or the threat that they will), making you fear loneliness

✓ Helplessness over painful situations, and afraid to feel the pain you've felt before

✓ Someone discounting or ignoring you, making you feel unworthy

✓ Someone being unavailable to you, as if you're unimportant

✓ Someone giving you a disapproving look, that makes you feel less than

✓ Someone blaming or shaming you, reminding you of a previous event

✓ Someone being judgmental or critical of you, making you feel small

✓ Someone being too busy to make time for you, like you're insignificant

✓ Someone not appearing to be happy to see you, and you wonder why

✓ Someone coming on to you sexually in a needy way, like you're an object

✓ Someone trying to control you, making you feel vulnerable

✓ Someone being needy or trying to smother you,

making you want to flee

Most people feel their trigger whenever someone expresses any disapproval of them. Suddenly, a simple comment can leave us feeling off-center and thrust into a bout of anxiety, depression, guilt, or shame. We immediately become uncomfortable, defensive, and our whole being is thrown out of kilter, as our emotions collide, and we search for ways to deal with our typhoon of feelings. Knowing our triggers allows us to watch for them, head them off, and deal with them before they overtake us. Our spouses should also know our triggers, and for the same reasons.

• • •

Part of communication includes showing gratitude to our partners for what they do and who they are in our world. Receiving appreciation fulfills a basic human need, and it's something so simple to give to our partners. Showing gratitude and appreciation doesn't even take words. Actions can sometimes speak volumes. Little things, like a fresh flower left on our partner's windshield for him to find or a heart drawn in lipstick on the bathroom mirror or taking the kids off our partner's hands for a much-needed break can say 'I'm thinking of you and I appreciate all you do for me!' It's the small, random acts that are always remembered, and it's these simple things that can change someone's entire outlook on life!

Our values and our character are parts of our makeup that we carry with us into the world. They're innate components of our constitution, and they're usually the things on which we base all decisions in our life. At the end of the day, if partners don't share the same values and are of similar character, they'll eventually have issues. Entrepreneurs take these things into their businesses too and use them to steer their decisions. Most times, when a couple has found one another, they've identified some similar values that are at the core of all they do. When communicating, reflect on those core values and the character traits of your mate. Chances are, you'll realign with him and feel more grounded when you remember what you share with your partner or spouse.

Entrepreneurs know that standing still and not embracing change is the most definite way to end their business. The same can be said for marriage. Expect change, especially in our immediate-gratification, high-tech society. If change throws fear into your heart, talk about it with your spouse. Discuss what really scares you about the change and what can be done to alleviate those fears. The main reason people resist change is that they fear what it will mean. Sometimes though, change brings with it a world of opportunity that's just waiting to be tapped! Embrace change and all the possibilities that come with it!

As you're communicating, evolving, and learning about your partner, remember always to put him first. This humble approach leads us to be compassionate and considerate in all we do. It doesn't mean putting ourselves last or not being heard. It's not a sacrifice or a negative thing at all. It just means thinking about our partner before ourselves. Do it and watch how your partner or spouse mirrors it back to you! The act makes people want to do the same and to share the positive feelings that he's felt. It's a consideration that always has positive results for both the giver and the recipient, and the residual effects benefit all those around us.

*"Your life unfolds in proportion to your courage."*
—*Unknown*

# WE ARE RESPONSIBLE FOR THE ENERGY WE BRING

S INCE I WANTED TO learn more about how to communicate with my husband and how my thoughts, actions,
and behaviors influenced the energy around me, I learned
about NLP or Neurolinguistic programming. Originated in the
1970's, NLP explores the link between communication and
personal development and how our language and behavioral
patterns affect our success in all areas of life. In a nutshell,
NLP seeks to show how 'what we put out into the universe
affects what we get back.' Created by two California psycho-
therapists, NLP has been used to treat things like depression,
phobias, and psychosomatic illnesses, but it's also embraced
by people who simply want to improve their communication
skills, body language, and the image they present to the world.
It is used by individuals and companies alike and is sometimes implemented in leadership training seminars to teach
people how to better relate to others, starting with the image
they present.

During an NLP session, I learned that the energy we create,
whether from positive or negative vibes, radiates from us to
about ten feet. I thought about this and realized that it's true.
Think for a moment about the impatient man in the bank line
that keeps checking his watch, shifting his weight between
both feet, and making faces at the teller. His negative vibe

says he's clearly in a bad mood, feeling inconvenienced, and not very approachable. His energy acts almost like a repellant that tells people to 'stand clear.' Or consider the overwrought mother in the grocery store, with a crying infant in the cart's seat and a tired toddler whining for a box of sugary cereal that's at eye level. She's irritated, probably overtired, and in need of a break, even a small one. Without a single word, it's clear what's going on in the situation. Similarly, if you see a kindly grandmother on a park bench, with a twinkle in her eye and a ready smile, you feel compelled to look her in the face and say, "Good morning!" or perhaps even take a seat beside her and strike up a chat. Her energy is warm, welcoming, and encouraging you to move closer and bask in it, maybe soak up a bit for yourself!

Have you ever been around someone and felt uncomfortable or like you don't want to be near them? Did you feel that the energy they were radiating made the entire room feel 'off' in some way like a gray cloud had been cast over it? Was your first thought that you should avoid the person or move away from them? It was the energy that they communicated that gave your brain the cues about how to react, almost like a 'fight or flight' response. This is particularly important for a marriage and for business relationships too since 'people' are involved. Since Matt and I work together, eat all meals together, and even shower together, we are together most of the time. Luckily, we love it and it works for us. Some people might say, "I would go crazy if I had to spend that much time with my spouse!" I get that, but it is what we do, and we feel blessed to have this kind of marriage.

But we've had to work to understand one another, what we each want, what our spouse wants, and how to sometimes compromise and make things work. All marriages, even all relationships, have compromises from time to time. But when both parties work toward making the arrangement work, everyone wins in the end.

...

Over the years, as I mentioned earlier, I've learned that I have triggers, those little things that evoke visceral reactions within me. We *all* do. Have you ever had something that was said or happened and you begin to feel this pull that starts in your stomach and rises through your chest, sometimes stopping in your throat, where it gets stuck? It makes you react in a defensive or sometimes hurtful way? You're affected by an action of another that brought back a feeling or emotion from your past. It's an abundance of smoldering energy that collects and it simply *must* escape your body; therefore, we react, frequently in a powerful eruption that wreaks havoc on those closest to us. Depending upon the situation, and what else has been going on, I can sometimes become quiet, pull back, and withdraw from my emotions. But they're still trapped inside me, alternately boiling and simmering, just waiting for the lid to pop off and release them. Other times, I may say something snarky or passive-aggressive, or worst-case scenario, I may have a slow climb flip out. "What is a slow climb flip out?" you may ask. Well, it is when that ball of energy collects and grows inside my stomach, and then slowly rises up into my chest until I react with gigantic, overt theatrical emotions. (Picture an ocean as a tidal wave forms, ominously churning and threatening to overtake an entire civilization. It's like *that*.) When such a trigger comes from a sensitive and dangerous internal place, it makes the reaction hugely intense.

My brain cannot reset itself until all the negative energy (aka 'reaction') is released. I think of it as a spiral; I feel out of control and super emotionally charged, almost like an alternative energy force that could sustain our planet for the next year.

Such reaction is really our body's way of protecting us. When something happens and our brain recalls a painful feeling or uncomfortable memory, it is just nudging us to say, "Hey, be careful!" The red, flashing, warning lights flash internally within us—but frequently, those who know us best see the external warning signs too and they have their reactions to that threatening tidal wave that's gaining strength. Through NLP, I'm learning to quiet that inner alarm and to let my brain know 'I'm okay, and there is no need to bring those painful memories to the surface or throw up defenses and overt reactions.' Thanks to my NLP sessions, I've learned that energy, both positive and negative, affects everyone around me. People that know me best have noticed the change within me and many have said, "Wow! I need to work on that too!"

• • •

*We* are responsible for the energy we bring. It radiates from us and can affect others around us. If we recognize within ourselves negative vibes and we find ourselves in an ugly, negative, or destructive mental place, it's best to push the reset button and organize our thoughts and feelings before they overtake our emotions. It takes practice, but it can be done, and I'm living proof. Once we recognize the negative feelings, the next step is to get control of them. It's done through breathing techniques, meditation, prayer, changing our perspectives, or anything else that works to interrupt the negative feelings and get control over them.

Different methods work for different people, and sometimes it's necessary to try several techniques to find what works best. First, make a conscious effort to surround yourself with positive people, those people who always 'see the glass half-full' and look at the bright sides of things. Realize that you do have control and it's up to you as to how you react. When something bothers you, no matter how big or small, change the way you look at the situation. Growth starts from within; therefore, it's up to you to decide how you'll react and how you'll allow something to affect you.

Don't take everything so seriously. Realize that it's okay to laugh at yourself now and then. Sometimes people look to us to see how we'll react in situations, and they then mirror their reactions based on ours. This is an opportunity to set the mood and control how a situation turns out.

Laughter really can be the best medicine. Lighten the mood and change your outlook simply by laughing. But laughter's value is so much more than just that! Laughter is an antidote to pain, both physical and mental, conflict, anger, and stress. It lessens burdens, changes the mood, makes us approachable, and even makes us appear more youthful and rested. In the moment, laughter makes us feel better by releasing endorphins. When people see or hear us laugh, they automatically smile and laugh too. As a result, the positive effects are exponentially shared. Laughing today can even help us tomorrow. Laughter boosts the immune system by decreasing stress hormones and increasing infection-fighting antibodies that help ward off sickness. Laughter is a simple gift you can give to your mind and body, and it's something you can share with everyone, yet it won't cost you a dime!

Changing our perspectives allows us to view situations from another vantage point. When faced with something uncomfortable, take a moment, step back, and decide if it's really a big deal, as compared to other things in your life. In a few years, will it really matter?

Another way to change our perspective is to think of all the good things we have in life. Gratitude has a way of immediately restoring balance in our life and reminding us of all we have and of what we hold dear. In comparison to all the good things in our life, a momentary situation suddenly becomes much less substantial and of little consequence. Besides, whatever has darkened our mood is usually just a temporary condition that will pass, and when it does, we'll still be grateful for all the good things and blessings in our life.

Since we are responsible for the energy we bring to a situation, it's so much more beneficial to bring light, positive, happy energy! Even better, when we are positive, those around us come toward us, eager to stand in the light with us and benefit in the reflection of our positive energy. Good things are born out of positivity. Relationships thrive, people are more effective and more efficient. They are naturally more agreeable, and therefore, easier to deal with almost all the time, and they take away a positive, favorable impression of us. This is important because while people may forget what we say or do, they rarely forget how we made them feel. They will, therefore, associate us with positive feelings and eagerly anticipate our next communication or meeting.

• • •

My marriage is precious to me, a gift from God that I protect above all else. I honor it, protect it, and value it more than anything. But none of us knows what tomorrow may bring, or even if we'll be blessed *with a tomorrow*. That's why I choose to make today the best it can be. I can only control myself and how I react to situations, circumstances, and people. As I've learned and grown, I've made a conscious choice to be *the best me I can be*.

# 9
# ACHIEVING FREEDOM THROUGH LIFE BALANCE

SOME PEOPLE REALLY have no idea why they do what they do, day after day. Ask why they work at their job and most people will say it's to provide for their families or to pay their bills. But, ask an entrepreneur why he owns his own business, and chances are, he'll have a bigger answer. Most entrepreneurs choose to work for themselves, not just to get rich, but to enjoy freedom in their life. The ultimate freedom comes not from an accumulation of wealth, but from life balance.

Loving your work is a gift, but loving your work also makes it easy to neglect other parts of your life. Entrepreneurs decide where their time goes, who gets to share in it, and how it'll be used. They understand that time is a commodity that once used up can never be replaced. Therefore, entrepreneurs seek to balance their dual identities and their business and personal lives to get the most out of all areas.

Achieving life balance is liberating, but it is also a tremendous responsibility. 'Time freedom' and 'financial freedom' are frequent words spoken in the entrepreneurial arena. The desire for this freedom can make us say 'yes' a lot more than we should. But there are still just twenty-four hours in a day—even for an entrepreneur. That's why life balance is so critical.

*Do you ever think, "If I could just connect with the right person, launch this next big project, or secure the next big deal, then I can slow down?"*

Successful people are always looking toward the next milestone, the bigger deal, the highest-profile client, or the major account they want to land.

Meanwhile, the clock continues to tick, and the calendar continues to flip. Time waits for no one, not even entrepreneurs. That is why achieving life balance is especially important for people who work for themselves, with no set hours and no specific workdays. Entrepreneurship IS a lifestyle. It doesn't just affect our lifestyle. Knowing how to navigate the lifestyle provides the best returns, both personally and professionally.

For those in corporate America, they work toward retirement, the time when they get to slow down and do the things they enjoy. Maybe it's traveling, fly fishing, painting, or golfing that they love and that they can't wait to do three times a week 'after they retire.' Entrepreneurs enjoy similar things, but since entrepreneurship is their lifestyle, they must figure out a way to do all the things they love. To do that, they must figure out a life balance that works for them and their families.

Being an entrepreneur and working for oneself admittedly has many perks. But when his company is new, there's no one to pick up the slack, no one who can 'cover for him' if he's sick, and no one to go to when problems arise. Any entrepreneur will tell you that he's never worked longer or harder in his life than when he worked for himself. Without life balance though, he'd fail at something, in either his personal life, his business life, or even both areas.

When one works a J.O.B, the game is to hustle, and put in the time, effort, and sacrifice, so that in thirty years or so, he can retire, slow down, and finally enjoy what's left of his life. An entrepreneur hustles, sacrifices, and puts in incredible amounts of time, but he realizes that time stands still for no one, so he looks for ways to live today and on his own terms. His definition of success doesn't come in the form of a gold watch, but rather in the fact that he gets to live life doing whatever he wants, whenever he chooses.

> *Have you ever heard someone say, "I will grind, hustle, work twenty hours a day, travel several times a month to events, be away from my family, and then one day I will be able to slow down and finally enjoy life!"?*

That does not appeal to most people, not in the least. Does that sound like freedom? Is that what the freedom that we desire looks like? Is that the freedom we post about on Facebook, that we pimp out to the world? The problem I see with this is there is always more to do, more to get, more to reach, and more to BE in life. It'll always be more deals, more connections, more events, more revenues, more goals, more, more, more! We decide where our time goes, right? The responsibility for us to show up, to present to our friends and family a less frazzled and less stressed-out version of ourselves is crucial. It must come first before we can attain the freedom that we seek.

Children have the inherent ability to know when they need to rest. I can find my kids anywhere in the house and passed out at any given the time of day. They simply stop playing and put their heads down and give their bodies and minds a rest.

Yet as adults, we ignore ourselves; we ignore the little tugs and cries from our inner voice. We find it difficult to say 'no,' to turn off our computers, to put our phones on 'silent,' and to give ourselves a well-deserved break. But for how long can we do this without suffering for our decisions?

Loving what you do is amazing and important but striving for balance and taking care of ourselves is just as important as freedom. True freedom can only be enjoyed when life balance is achieved and creating it sooner than later may be the deciding factor in whether we're here to enjoy our families in the coming years.

No one wants to be a caged hamster on a wheel, running, running, running, with no destination in sight. Yet that's what many people do, day after day, and without question. Even if they don't like their jobs or their lives, they still stay on the wheel and continue to put one foot in front of the other, without changing course or altering their pace. If they had balance in their lives, they'd see that there's more to life than just the grind and hustle of a job.

*Why go through the repetitive exercise if you can't enjoy life along the way?*

How will you feel if you finally get to your destination, but you're too worn out to enjoy it and bask in the fruits of your labor? Will your partner be waiting for you at the finish line if he's felt excluded, neglected, and avoided while you ran the race and chased your dream?

• • •

Achieving life balance starts with each one of us, and it includes making the best decisions in each area of our lives. I once read a post from a young woman who's an entrepreneur, and it tugged at my heart. She was asking for people in the entrepreneurial space to be real. She'd been up all night with a sick child, and when her child finally fell asleep, the woman went onto Facebook to relax for a few minutes. She saw people posting about 'the hustle' and 'doing whatever it takes, no matter what,' and she immediately felt defeated. But I ventured to guess that many of those who posted had not walked in this young woman's shoes. They probably didn't know what it was like to have a feverish, overtired toddler on their lap, with a cell phone to their ear, as they sat, un-showered and exhausted, in front a computer screen discussing the proposal they'd submitted to the client on the other end of the phone. While, of course, their child is the most important thing, so is paying the mortgage for that child's home; therefore, the client's business is an integral part of the harried mother's world too. If the mother worked for another employer, she'd likely have 'paid sick days,' and so she could've called in sick that day and then focused her full attention on her child. But that's not how it is for an entrepreneur.

Most entrepreneurs will say, "What IS a sick day anyway?" because such things are luxuries not frequently enjoyed by the self-employed—at least not in the early days of their businesses. That's why it's sometimes amusing when people use terms like 'the hustle' and 'doing whatever it takes.' That young woman who'd been up all night with her ill child had most likely done those things and more—and yet she still felt defeated. She was still searching for and working on creating life balance in her world. Days like she'd had sound very familiar to entrepreneurs and for the ones who have achieved life balance, they never want to go back to days like the one the young woman had described!

I suspect that the young woman found her way and figured out to find a balance in her life. Entrepreneurs are a resourceful and hardy bunch that don't easily give up on their dreams. It takes sacrifice to build something amazing, but eventually, life balance must be found. Without it, burnout always follows.

The young woman had her priorities straight. She put her child first and taking care of her client was also taking care of her child's needs. We sometimes forget what the hustle and sacrifice can do to the people in our lives. It can leave family members feeling unimportant, unloved, alone, misunderstood, and scared. It can make the people watching feel like they're not doing, sacrificing, and 'hustling and grinding' enough, as compared to the multi-tasking entrepreneur. 'The Hustle' has become a badge of honor, proudly worn and displayed to show the world that 'we do what it takes' and that 'we've got what it takes.' But are we truly being honest about the casualties and the fallout that are the result of that journey? Being real in this space can make one feel vulnerable, but there is so much power in that vulnerability. When men hear the word 'vulnerability,' they frequently associate it with 'weakness,' but what vulnerability means is that there's possibility for growth and change. Since evolution, men usually don't like to be 'vulnerable,' as if it has a negative connotation. But when embraced, vulnerability opens us up to new possibilities and better ways of doing things. It's not an imperfection; it's a step toward improvement.

Allowing ourselves to be vulnerable is the first step toward life balance because it makes us take a long, hard look at ourselves, our ambitions, our relationships, and yes, even our flaws and shortcomings. It always leads us toward empathy, which is what connects us to others, and no matter our roles in life or in our businesses, we all must deal with people. This includes spouses, children, families, friends, clients, employees, and even the barista that sees us every morning as we head into work!

For just one day, slow down, be vulnerable, and empathize with each and every person with whom you come in contact. Take an extra two seconds and make eye contact with the server that brings your breakfast and ask how she's been, ask the postman how he's handling the recent weather, talk with employees about their plans for the holidays, and inquire about your neighbor's spouse that you haven't seen in a while. Watch how you literally feel your core open up and invite those people into your space and notice how they appear lighter, happier, and grateful that you took the time to see them, to really see them. The exchange enhances their day, makes you vulnerable to conversation, to feelings, and to their opinions of you.

But don't stop there. Do the same with your spouse and your children. Don't just say, "How was your day?" Ask a question that invites open conversation and an exchange of ideas. If your spouse had an important presentation that day, specifically say, "Tell me about how your talk went today." This ensures that a fluid conversation will take place. It opens you up or makes you vulnerable to your spouse. Feel the connection that is established in the next couple of minutes as he or she talks about their day. Even better, it sets the tone for the rest of the evening, because the two of you have already opened communications and there's a conduit that invites more dialogue. After doing this for a few evenings, you may not even reach for the TV remote or open your laptop, instead opting to talk and share with your spouse. The effects will be exponential and long-lasting, if only you take the first step and open yourself to vulnerability and walk toward the life balance you seek!

Assumption and a lack of communication is a relationship killer. To achieve life balance, we must take into consideration our spouse's feelings and thoughts. We must make them an integral part of all we do. After all, we're together with them because they're the most important person in our life, right? It's easy to become so invested in our pursuit of success that we get distracted from the reason we do what we do, the core of all we hold dear in life. Take the time, make an effort, and solidify the bond, and continue to do these things, again and again. After all, what is success if you're not with your spouse when you've found it?

• • •

Do not fast-forward to a place in the future that you haven't yet earned. It's a recipe for failure, and you'll never find the life balance that'll make you feel fulfilled and successful. It is true that success happens if a journey and all the miles we walk hold lessons. If you try to fast-forward to a place not yet earned, you'll arrive without the lessons, and you'll most definitely slide backward and be forced to walk the journey that you skipped.

How many times have you tried to get to a place in your business or your personal life for which you weren't ready?

Chances are, you couldn't hold onto the place you'd reached, and it didn't feel quite as good since you skipped over some of the places in the journey on your rush to arrive. For me, this held true for my business. I wanted it, all of it, immediately! I sometimes tried to put myself in places that, if I'm honest, I was not at all ready to be. What resulted was that things didn't work out in my favor, and only I ended up hurting myself in the process.

There were times in Matt's and my life when we'd tried to live a certain way or do certain things that were not purposefully aligned with that stage of our journey. It wasn't like those things weren't in our future, but they just weren't meant for our present. It was like we wanted certain things so badly that we hurried up and forced our way in, and I promise that there hasn't been a time that those tactics worked out for us.

I see this sort of behavior a lot. People live beyond their means, doing things they wouldn't normally do because they so desperately want to be in a place that would reflect the lifestyle they desire. But they just aren't ready to be there yet, so the universe has a way of forcing them to slip back and travel the road, one step at a time until they earn the lifestyle they desire. They may arrive a little more battered, tired, and scathed, but when they get there, after taking the longer route, the destination is so much sweeter!

Timing is everything in almost all areas of life. There's a certain degree of bumps, struggles, hard times, and mountain climbing to be experienced to obtain anything worthwhile. There are a few exceptions to this, but the key word is exceptions.

Matt sometimes reminds me, when I get frustrated, that 'things aren't moving as fast as I would like for my business and that I have to earn it.' He says to not be in a hurry. This, of course, isn't what I want to hear. The little voice in my head asks, "Why should I struggle when my husband is so successful, and he has the tools needed to move me along, without all the heartache he experienced along the way?" And I then agree and silently think, "That's right! Why should I struggle when I have the coolest connections that are doing extraordinary things?" The answer, to be frank, is that I haven't earned my spot yet. I haven't walked every step of the journey that will lead me toward my desired place. If I don't walk every pace of the journey, a step at a time, I'll never attain the life balance I seek. It's simply not possible since my place in the universe will be off-balance and out of kilter. Realizing this put me one step closer to the summit, to the destination I saw on the horizon!

· · ·

Achieving life balance doesn't only mean balancing work, career, and family. It also includes balancing our minds, our hearts, and our spirits. To some, it may seem like a gigantic, unattainable thing that they can never possibly reach, let alone even imagine. But by taking a step-by-step approach, anyone can find it.

Years ago, we'd look at a big, unfolded roadmap and figure out how to get from our home to the desired destination. Finding life balance is like that practice. First, consider where you are in life right now, this minute, and then envision where you'd ultimately like to be. Visualize the perfect life that you desire, the lifestyle where you should be and where you feel that you ultimately belong. The path in between those two points is the route you will travel as you seek your destination.

Next, consider all the areas of your life, including personal, family, career, financial, and spiritual. Each of these areas must be considered along with your journey to life balance. If you ignore even one of the areas, you'll be detoured on your trip and your journey will take longer to complete.

Make a list of all the areas in your life. Under each area, note how you contribute to enhancing or promoting each facet. (Hint: Honesty counts.) If you're not doing enough in one area, it's better to own it, acknowledge it, and work on it. Ignoring it or being dishonest about how you contribute in an area will only stall your progress on the journey. Reflect on what you've done in the past year toward enhancing each of the areas in your life. Working on the areas means you're making progress. Next, consider what else you can do to advance in each area of your life. Write down under each area what you plan to do to ensure you keep progressing.

Mental preparation is imperative to making progress, so prepare yourself mentally for the journey ahead. Let go of or resolve any old issues, bad feelings, or self-doubts you've harbored in the past. They'll only act as gigantic boulders on the road to finding life balance. If you can't remove these obstacles, the journey takes much longer!

Next, consider your resources, those persons or connections that can help you to find the balance and the lifestyle you seek. This might be a spouse, a colleague, a friend, a mentor, a pastor, or even someone whose life's success you admire. These people are a huge resource, and they hold a wealth of information that can propel you toward finding the life you want. After you've identified your resources, consider how each can assist you in your journey. Chances are, these people have had help from others too and they'll feel compelled to help you as they've been helped along on their paths toward success.

Chart your progress in the journey! As you gain ground, make strides, and take steps toward your goals, keep track of your progress. It'll be a motivator, especially when you run into roadblocks now and then. As you begin to see each area of your life find a new balance, you'll also feel your whole world has also found a balance. Before long, you'll find yourself at the destination you first plotted when you set out on your trip to the lifestyle you initially desired. All journeys begin with a first step!

*"True love is an act of the will—a conscious decision to do what is best for the other person instead of ourselves."*

*—Billy Graham*

# 10

# LOCKER ROOM CONFESSIONS

SOMETIMES WE ARE meant to be in a certain spot at a precise time. One morning, while I was in the locker room at the gym, I overheard a conversation that made me feel sad, and at the same time, it made me feel thankful. As I changed clothes, there were two ladies discussing retirement. During their conversation, one of them mentioned that she recently had to spend a week with her husband at a hotel.

"I don't know how I'll survive retirement with him!" she exclaimed. "I can't imagine having to be around him all the time! I mean, I love him and all, but..."

"I know exactly what you mean," agreed the other woman. "When I had to spend a month with my husband, I nearly lost my mind! I love my husband too, but it was awful, just awful!"

I continued dressing, but I turned my back so that the ladies wouldn't see the expression of shock on my face.

"With John's career, I pretty much just stay busy with the house, the kids, and everything, while he does his thing," the first woman added. "And when he comes home at night, it's dinner, bedtime, and getting ready for the next day."

"I know what you mean. We really only have to spend time with them on the weekends and holidays," Number Two interjected.

"Exactly," Number One agreed.

My mind was spinning as I tried to digest what I'd just overheard. "Did I hear just hear that correctly?" I thought. "These lovely ladies are dreading having to spend time with their spouses, the very men they married and promised to love forever?"

It genuinely saddened me to hear the ladies' comments. I'm certainly not naive to the fact that this is how many long-married couples feel. It's not the first time I'd heard such conversation, and not only from wives, but I'd also heard similar talk from husbands. It just seemed so sad.

As Matt and I drove home from the gym together, I told him about what I'd heard. We began to dissect the reasons that so many people come to have such feelings. Why do married couples feel this way? How do they get to this place? Our conversation also made me look at myself. Matt and I have had our share of marital strife, and the ladies' conversation was a reminder of how empty the love tank can get without the proper care and maintenance. The person that these ladies had a distaste for is also the very same person that they once stood in front of and promised their forever love.

I believe that such feelings evolve from a lack of being present, not only in the marriage but to one's self's needs and wants. I have been with Matt for fifteen years. I'm not entirely the same person that I was fifteen years ago. I have changed and evolved as a woman. Sure, my values and basic moral fiber have remained the same, but my likes, dislikes, and some of my beliefs have changed significantly and so have Matt's for that matter. We had to be present and appreciate where the other person was in their life's journey. Did we nail this every time over the years? No, not at all, but the effort was made and continues to be made, and sometimes 'just knowing' that our spouse puts forth the effort is all that's needed.

Similarly, I also believe that the effort made toward one other can die off or fizzle out if we let it. For instance, think about how we treat our friend. We make an effort to be a good friend, to let our friends know they're important and valuable. We treat our friends with love. We give them the benefit of the doubt, we laugh easily at their jokes, we show them respect, and we always greet them with smiles and affection that lets them know we're pleased to see them.

*Why then would we not do the same for our spouse?*

*Aren't they our best friends, the most significant other in our world, and the one individual around whom our world is centered?*

All most people want is to be seen, heard, acknowledged, and valued. Whether those people are our friends or our spouses, their basic needs yearn to be met. Think of how it was in the early days of your relationship, those sunny, exhilarating times when the exhilaration of hearing your man's (or woman's) voice on the phone set your heart aflutter. The anticipation of seeing your mate filled you with excitement and promise, and when your dates ended, you immediately began counting down the hours till you'd meet again! The way you felt when you were away from your mate was what made you know you couldn't live without him!

Marriage does not have to be a chore. In fact, it is a huge blessing. We do not have to fall into the socially accepted norm of referring to our spouse as 'a ball and chain.' We can have a happy, love-filled relationship, still filled with wonder, excitement, and promise!

Most women will agree that they find it sexy when guys are devoted husbands that put their wives first. It's doubly attractive when men are involved, loving fathers. Matt says, "The best way to be good to your children is to be good to their mother." Is it always easy to do that? No. Is it necessary to be selfless to put the other first? Yes. But just as we dedicate ourselves to the success of our business, we can also dedicate ourselves to the success of our marriage.

I readily admit that I've made many mistakes as a wife. I have tripped, fallen, and sometimes landed hard. When it comes to doing the right thing, I have, at times, been far less than perfect. Matt and I have hurt each other and been hurt by each other. But forgiveness and grace were given and accepted and I thank God for that!

Like everyone, I get overwhelmed, overtired, and even irritable at times. These are the times when I stop, breathe, and refocus my feelings and remember what's important. These are the times that I must count my blessings and remember just how far we've come and the hurdles we've overcome— together. I'm grateful that I get to spend every day with my husband. I'm thankful we are both on our own personal growth journeys and that we each seek to be better in all areas of our lives. These are gifts we give ourselves, but also each other. I believe that God gives me moments of reflection as reminders of my priorities, so I can make the best choices that will support those priorities.

A beautiful, flowering garden draws people nearer. They want to see the beauty up close, they want to inhale the sweet fragrances, and they sometimes want to even pick a few flowers to take with them, so they can continue to enjoy how the garden made them feel. It's obvious when a garden is tended, watered, fertilized, pruned, and weeded. Without speaking a word, a tended garden says, 'Someone cares about me and spends time making sure I have all I need.' But the contrary can also ring true. If a garden is left untended, and no one waters it, feeds it, or weeds it, it soon becomes a tangled, dying, unattractive, undesirable heap of withering and dying flowers. This is exactly what happens when we fail to tend or take care of our marriages. Little by little, it becomes obvious that no one is tending and nurturing the marriage. This is when the marriage is even more vulnerable to outside pests and predators. In its weakened state, the marriage is easily trampled, infected, and killed off.

I know from personal experience how empty a marriage can feel when we stop taking care of it. It first becomes stagnant, and in time, it can sour, stink, and even altogether dry up. It becomes barren and infertile, unable to sustain or support either spouse. Left untended, the marriage shrivels and eventually turns to dust. The saddest part is that most marriages can be mended, strengthened, and saved if only both parties do their parts to work on it.

In many cases, the best place to start such work can be found 'in the mirror.' When we are not happy with ourselves, and not living joyously, it's easy to let the seeds of cynicism and angst take root. The strength in joy and positivity acts almost like a protective shield because it reminds us what's good in life and for what we are most thankful. Without such a mindset, those negative seeds grow into the weeds that will choke out and eventually kill a marriage. When negativity and doubt water those seeds, the result creates a dangerous combination. For this reason, it's important to be careful who we allow to be our sounding boards, especially when we're in a weakened, vulnerable state.

While the health of a marriage is the responsibility of both parties, each has his own responsibility to be happy. It is not our spouse's job to make us happy or to give us joy. Happiness is an inside job, something that we create and invoke inside ourselves. If we do not have this, then it is our responsibility to seek it, pray for it, and work for it. The burden does not fall on our partner, and it's impossible to grow and to live fully or joyously without it.

To some, being happy and living with joy may sound like a tall order, so tall, in fact, that some people don't know where to start to find it, or even where to look first. When life comes at us from all directions, and we feel overwhelmed and flummoxed, what we really need is to refocus and gain perspective over the 'big picture' of our life. There are several things we can do when we need to refocus and realign our priorities in our busy world.

Gratitude always puts things in order and slows us down, so we can savor the good things in life, all those things for which we're so thankful. Gratitude is a very personal thing, and there's no right or wrong way to acknowledge, feel, or show it. Surprisingly, studies of how gratitude correlates with psychology only came to light around the year 2000. Earlier psychological studies concentrated more on distressed psyches and how to deal with their results, instead of looking at how positive psychological exercises might prevent such negative outcomes. Studies have shown that positive, sometimes preemptive, behaviors can have immediate and long-lasting influences on a person's overall emotional state. The benefits are sometimes felt exponentially in a sort of 'infectious' way that shares the positivity with others.

Gratitude really does affect attitude! So, how can you start to positively affect your attitude and the attitudes of those around you? It can be as simple or as complex as you'd like. As an experiment, start small and keep it basic and then watch how the results change your outlook and affect your whole day! Since we all have different lives, unique circumstances, and underlying issues, it's safe to assume that we have various perspectives about aspects of our lives. Still, though, each of us has things, both big and small, for which we are grateful. Create a new, positive habit and start each day with gratitude. Some people choose to do this as soon as they open their eyes, the first time they look in the mirror each morning, or during their morning commute to work. Choose the time that's best for you and your schedule. Begin the statement the same each day and fill in the blank with whatever first enters your mind. Say:

**I am grateful for** _____.

Speak the words, put the gratitude into the atmosphere, and allow it to radiate around you. Maybe you're grateful for your spouse or your family, your good health, a new promotion at work, or simply the beautiful sunrise that brought with it the promise of new possibilities. As you begin to name things for which you're grateful, you'll soon see all the positive things in your life. Sure, you'll still have stresses, worries, and fears, but your perspective will shift and you'll bask in gratitude for the good things life has given to you. There is power in this positive affirmation that'll take you through your day and give you the extra 'Oomph!' you'll need to carry on!

No matter how bad things may get, and no matter how overwrought you may feel, this gratitude affirmation will change the way you look at life. Take the time to note and reflect upon all the things for which you're thankful and then notice how you feel empowered, invigorated, more vibrant, less stressed, more compassionate, and kinder. The results are not only emotional either. Studies have shown that we even sleep better, have stronger immune systems, and enjoy better health when we begin to look at life with gratitude and give thanks for all we do have, instead of ruminating about what our life lacks.

Another great way to start the day is with positive affirmations. This can also be difficult to do, at first, but it gets easier when the benefits are realized! Daily affirmations really work! Just like Zig Zigler once declared that "Doing something 21 times makes it a habit," we can also create a positive habit by doing daily affirmations. Affirmations are as unique as snowflakes and finding the right ones is critical to our success and even our happiness! There are a ton of affirmations out there that you can adopt, or you can create one that's unique to your issues and needs.

To find the right affirmation for you, first decide if you'd like to focus on relationships, health, career, self-esteem, body image, or any other area in which you'd like to improve. Create a simple affirmative sentence that speaks to you on a personal level. A few examples might be:

*I am all I need.*

*I am strong, and I can live without fear.*

*I am a gift to this world.*
*I enjoy my own company.*
*Only my opinion of myself matters.*
*I trust myself to make the right decisions.*
*I forgive myself for past mistakes.*
*I am filled with courage.*
*I love my family even if we are different.*
*I am a better person for all my hardships.*
*Only I can influence my life.*
*I am unique, smart, and beautiful.*
*My gifts change the world.*
*I release the worries and stresses that burden and drain me.*
*I am a good person and I will do good in the world.*

When you decide on an appropriate daily affirmation, write it down and put it in a place where you'll see it every day. Depending upon your routine, the best place might be on your refrigerator, the bathroom mirror, on the visor in your car, or beside your computer. Place it in a spot where you'll see it throughout the day. Each time you view it, repeat the affirmation to yourself.

Many people find that this simple change realigns their perspective, improves their confidence, and helps motivate and guide them. The interesting thing is that as we affirm things to ourselves, others also begin to see those things in us too! Some people choose to use this technique as a self-improvement tool as they seek to change their lives. It's simple, inexpensive, and not time-consuming. No matter their affirmations, people report feeling more positive and powerful when they utilize the affirmations.

Just remember that affirmations don't erase our flaws and they don't mean we are perfect. They simply allow us to accept ourselves in our imperfection while we strive to improve ourselves. The mindful technique brings us closer to ourselves and opens us up to new possibilities while empowering us to move forward in life.

# A SOUND
# STRUCTURE

# FIVE KEY COMPONENTS TO A RICH & FULFILLED LIFE

**(I want to thank Matt Stefanik for teaching me this strategy)**

EVERYONE WANTS TO have a rich and fulfilled life. But that can seem like a huge order for some people. Entrepreneurs know that finding such rewards is a step-by-step process that breaks down each area of their lives to create just the balance they seek in each area. The five key components to a rich and fulfilled life include:

**Health**

**Financial Security**

**Healthy Relationships**

**Meaningful Work**

**Play**

Depending upon one's unique goals and life plans, some of these components may bear different weight and importance than others, but rest assured that balance must exist between all areas to find optimum fulfillment in life. If we're working too much and neglecting our health, our life is off-balance. If we allow our relationships to suffer because we work fifteen-hour days in pursuit of financial security, our world feels out of kilter. If our work doesn't feel satisfying and important, it's difficult to throw ourselves fully into it, and the result is that we feel out of sorts, like we're floundering.

*So, how do we achieve balance in each of the five components so that we can enjoy a rich and fulfilled life?*

The answer to this requires taking the time to dissect each component and asking some basic questions about what we want out of life. It requires a heart-to-heart with ourselves and a bit of soul searching. Take out a sheet of paper and write down each key component of life, leaving a few spaces between each heading. Next, set your intentions for each category or component.

**There are two basic questions you must ask yourself when considering each component:**

*What do I want to happen?*

*How do I want to feel?*

Again, there are no right or wrong answers. The only thing that matters is honesty with yourself about what you want. For instance, in the Health component, perhaps you'd like to lose ten pounds, reduce stress, or even stop smoking. That's what you'd like to happen. If you do those things, you'll feel better, enjoy less stress, and possibly add a few years to your life expectancy. Maybe you've been feeling unfulfilled in your career and like you're not doing something important with your work. You'd like to find a career that feeds your soul, uses your gifts, and positively impacts the world. The result will allow you to feel gratified and as if you're making a valuable contribution to your efforts. Possibly you've felt angst about your overall financial security; and so, you need to create a second form of income, cut expenses, or make some changes in your life. The results would provide you with a sense of financial stability, less stress, and more peace. Relationships are a part of life, and yet, all relationships are not healthy or positive. Would your life be happier and less stressful if you didn't have to deal with certain persons? Would such a change allow you to focus on the good and positive relationships in your world? If so, the result would lighten your heart, improve your mood, and nourish those positive relationships that deserve your time and energy.

The point is, you must look individually at each of the five components in life, commit to what you'd like to attain in each area, and then make the necessary changes that will take you to your individual goals. These finite, specific changes will slowly begin to balance your life, one area at a time. The result will be a more satisfied, gratified 'you' that enjoys a rich, fulfilled life that you've created!

Because life is a journey, we must keep striving to better ourselves and what we do with our lives. As we change, so do our goals, visions, and dreams. This is how it's supposed to be, but we must embrace each stage of life with a zestful attitude and a prepared mind and heart. This means learning about ourselves and giving of ourselves. Since none of us has 'all the answers' in life, we naturally rely on others for their expertise and insights as to how they've navigated certain parts of their own lives. There's huge value in learning from others, even if we cannot apply all the things that others have done. Just knowing there are options gives us insights and serves as a catalyst for us to work on ourselves. It reinforces for us that there are possibilities that exist for us to change and grow in our space.

We all learn differently, just as we all assimilate and process data in different ways. It doesn't matter so much how you obtain the knowledge as much as the fact that you're open to it and that you receive it. For instance, sales reps who are on the road sometimes opt for audio self-help books or recordings of speakers that impart their words of wisdom while the reps have endless 'windshield time.' Business travelers sometimes prefer to read trade publications or motivational books during flights to make the most of their time during a workday. Busy moms may only find a half-hour a day to grab a self-improvement book, either while they wait in the car line after school or while their kids are at soccer practice. It makes no difference how the information is received, so long as we get it!

The same goes for physical activity too. All of us do not have the time, the luxury, or even the budget to carve out two hours a day at a local gym. But that doesn't mean we can't still exercise and yield the benefits of it, both physically and mentally. Chasing toddlers in the park, swimming with our kids, and even dancing or jumping on a trampoline with our preteens counts as exercise and we can enjoy the huge benefits of our exercise.

While working on our minds and our bodies, it's important that we also feed our souls and nourish our spirits. This is a personal area that may include religious practices, spending quiet time, meditating, doing yoga, or even exploring nature's bounty. When we're feeling overwhelmed or anxious, we can change those feelings just by going outdoors. Feeling the warm sun and the gentle breezes, hearing the birds in the trees, and smelling the fresh scents of flora and fauna have immediate restorative effects on our psyche. Try it sometime and notice how quickly your mood improves and how refreshed and energized you feel!

The following are a few suggestions for improving the key components in your life as you work toward creating a rich and fulfilled life:

# Reading or Listening to Self-Improvement Books:

These books can relate to business or personal growth. They help provide a renewed focus, inspire and motivate us, and even remind us that we're not alone. Choose times every day to read or listen to an audio book. Pick a time that works best for your personal schedule. For some people, this is first thing in the morning, after they drop off their kids at school or while they drive to work. Commuters often use their travel time to read or to listen to a chapter while on the way to or from the office. Some people get in a little time during their lunch break. Others take a book with them to their kids' ball practice or they get a chapter or two in after the kids are in bed each night.

---

**TIP:** Select a book that resonates with you and the type of personal or professional growth you seek. Commit to reading it daily as an investment in yourself! If you're not sure what books to choose, ask for recommendations from friends or colleagues or even read online reviews to find the best book for you and your goals.

---

# Physical Activity:

Physical activity doesn't always have to mean doing specific, regimented exercises and the effects of such actions don't just benefit our bodies. For many people, physical activity is what 'keeps them sane.' Rather than dreading exercise, reprogram your thoughts to look forward to physical activity and the benefits it'll bring! Whether this means going to the gym, taking an exercise class, walking around your neighborhood, or simply taking a break and 'dancing to the Oldies,' the physical and mental rewards can be attained.

Even a few minutes of physical activity can deliver a refreshed, invigorated feeling and a new, clear perspective. Not only does such activity physically change your health and your appearance, but it also releases 'feel good' chemicals, or endorphins, in your brain that scientifically have been proven to make you happy. But the benefits don't stop there! People who get regular physical activity report being less stressed, more focused, and more productive, and they even get more restful sleep.

---

**TIP:** Inactivity prompts our bodies to adjust our metabolism since it doesn't sense we need to use calories for energy. Being sedentary means we don't use our large muscle groups, especially the lower ones. The long-term effects of too much sitting can have detrimental results to our health and have even been linked to some major diseases. If you work at a desk, set the timer or alarm on your cell phone to remind you to get up and go for a walk at least once an hour.

---

## Explore Nature:

Nature really does have healing powers! Studies have shown that people who get outside and experience nature also have less anxiety, less stress, and less depression. One explanation for this might be that people who go outside more often also naturally absorb higher levels of Vitamin D which helps with staving off obesity, controlling hormonal imbalances, and regulating our sleep cycles, among other things. In today's busy, high-tech world, it's so important to remove ourselves from technology and reconnect with nature.

The simplicity and perfection of nature grounds us and redirects our focus away from our other problems, concerns, stresses, and worries. The reason for this is because nature speaks to multiple senses at the same time and replaces all that static within us with positive things. The warmth of the sunshine restores us and brightens our mood, the smell of the air, with hints of fresh flowers or newfallen rain, washes away our worries, and the singsong of birds, ducks, or crickets replaces the worries that race through our heads. All these sensory benefits combine to restore us and refocus us.

---

**TIP:** The next time you feel 'blah,' worried, stressed, or even over-tired, walk outside. Let go of all the negativity that weighed you down and absorb a little bit of nature's bounty. Watch how it changes your whole mood! Better still, when you go inside again, watch how much more productive you are with the rest of your day!

---

# Give Yourself Permission to Take a Break:

In our non-stop, instant gratification, high-tech world, we are reachable and 'on call' twenty-four hours a day, seven days a week. Entrepreneurs especially know this to be true since their businesses are their lifeblood and the thing on which their lives and lifestyles are built. But everyone deserves a break now and then! Since most of us live structured, scheduled lives, and since entrepreneurs' business and personal lives often mesh, it's easier to 'take a break' if it's scheduled for certain days and times. This includes short breaks throughout the day, breaks for family time, and longer breaks for holidays and vacations.

Some people find it best to schedule regularly recurring break times, and they block off their schedules at those times each day and each week. Maybe this is an hour in the mornings when you can take the kids, so your spouse has an hour to themselves. Perhaps it's every evening when you can take the dog for a walk and have your son accompany you so that you can talk about his day or maybe it's thirty minutes every evening when you sit alone on your dock and just 'breathe.' Everyone is different, and our unique needs and responsibilities are different too. The point is that it's okay to block off time to be alone or to spend uninterrupted time with your spouse or your kids. The phone can wait, emails will still be waiting in an hour, and text messages will be there too when you return to them!

---

**TIP:** Coordinate calendars with your spouse to schedule 'together time.' Block off 'alone time' for yourself, even if it's just fifteen minutes a day. Agree that during these times there are no phones, no computers, and no outside interruptions.

---

Each of the above suggestions relies on asking yourself the same two, basic questions first discussed at the beginning of this chapter:

*What do I want to happen?*

*How do I want to feel?*

When committing to implementing the suggestions, simply ask yourself those questions. The answers will lead you to the changes you need to make and the changes will then lead to the rich, fulfilled life you desire!

# THE COMPANY WE KEEP & HOW DO I MEASURE UP?

**I**T'S TRUE THAT we are judged by the company we keep. It's also true that we are influenced by the company we keep too. For better or for worse, our circle of influence has an impact on us, our perceptions, our motivations, our opinions, and our beliefs and actions. Just as we try to be wary of the people our kids are around, we should also be vigilant and selective about the people we let into our lives too.

We all need to have friends and family to whom we can turn in times of trial and during the good times. Be careful and choose wisely the people who you bring into your trusted circle. Be especially selective about the people you allow closest to the center of your circle, the nucleus, and the place that only you and your family can occupy.

Outer Circle

Inner Circle

My Spouse, My Family & Myself

Sometimes we place people too close to the center of our circle of influence when they really belong in the outer bands of the wider circle, and in the 'outer circle,' a more general position with less importance and less influence. Visualize yourself, your spouse, and your children in the center of your circle. Those persons closest to you and those you hold most dear should be the most trusted and important in your life. These persons are not always blood-related. They can be close friends whose trust and confidence has been earned over time. Beware of people who 'push' to be moved from the outer to the inner circle and understand their motives and intentions for wanting to be closer to you. Trust and friendship are earned, not freely given. Never be too eager to give them away or else you may find yourself in a precarious and vulnerable spot!

• • •

Theodore Roosevelt once said, "Comparison is the thief of joy," and he couldn't have been more correct. To stop comparing ourselves to others, we must first understand why we make the comparisons. It's natural to want to get ahead in life, pull away from the herd, and make a name for ourselves. For some people, this can't happen fast enough! But everything happens in its own time and we all progress at different speeds on our own unique journeys in life.

Studies show that humans compare themselves to others in an attempt to find their place or stature within the world and to better understand themselves. We mentally place ourselves on a sliding scale, and when we compare our life's progress, we may move up a notch or perhaps even slide backward a few notches. While it's not a bad thing to compare ourselves to our family, friends, or colleagues, it frequently leads to unproductive feelings, one way or the other. This is because it's nearly impossible to distance ourselves and gain a broader perspective of how we compare to others.

For instance, if we compare ourselves to our neighbor who just returned from a European vacation and is having a pool built, while he's got two brand-new luxury vehicles in his driveway, we might feel stressed that our budget doesn't currently allow for the same luxuries. If we, however, are that neighbor who's just returned from Paris and is having a pool built, while we're driving a new Maserati and a Range Rover, this might make us feel like we're doing better than others, but it could also lead to an unattractive vanity that repels people. The point is that it's unproductive to compare ourselves, no matter where we may fall on the social scale.

Remember that when we compare ourselves to others and their successes, we're only comparing ourselves to perceptions. Who's to say that the guy that looks like he has it all isn't also drowning in credit card debt? Maybe the family that appears to live lavishly is really pinching pennies to maintain the appearance of their success.

Perhaps the manicured, coiffed woman in designer clothes is miserable in life and hiding behind a façade of perfection. We only get a glimpse into the lives of others, just a snapshot into their worlds,and only what they want us to see. Scroll through social media accounts and notice how everyone's shared photos are of the good times. The pictures they show to the world are smiling, happy, celebratory ones in which they look their very best. But those same people may be dealing with stress, depression, financial worry, health concerns, and other negative issues.

To stop comparing ourselves to others means we've got to focus on ourselves and learn to love and accept ourselves for who we are and where we are in life. This is easier said than done, of course. But try putting that same thought and energy into working on yourself and watch how your focus changes and how you feel a new sense of pride and satisfaction in the life you've built. Comparing ourselves directs our energies in the wrong directions, and the outcomes are never gratifying. Sure, we all want to do well in life and reap the rewards of our efforts, but by focusing on our own lives, we direct all our efforts into working on us, instead of worrying about others.

This is another time when it's helpful to use positive affirmations to remind ourselves that 'we are enough' and 'we will succeed' in life. If comparing yourself to others is an issue, then create a positive affirmation that reinforces your vision. The results will empower and motivate you while redirecting your energies toward the positive results you seek.

Embrace the fact that 'you are unique,' and the only standards you must live up to are your own. You hold the measuring stick and the scale, and where others fall on it doesn't concern you or your progress in life. The goals you set are personal, and your life's journey is intimate. It's yours alone.

• • •

Our circle of influence is affected by how we compare ourselves to others and to the outside world, whether we want to admit it or not. We care what others think and about their perceptions of us. But this eventually becomes exhausting and counter-productive and it hinders our journey's progress. While we should care what our spouse thinks, the opinions of others are far less important in the grand scheme of things.

Are you only working hard so you can keep up with the Joneses? Of course not, so, reassess the priorities that govern your life. Throw that energy and time into working on your own path and focus on your journey. Comparing yourself to others can be painstakingly debilitating, even paralyzing at times. Feelings of inadequacy and inferiority creep in and overtake our psyches and thwart our progress. No matter how well you do in life, there will always be someone else who's doing better! So, let it go, and commit to stop comparing yourself!

This is when you'll really find value in those important persons within your circle of influence. The ones who are closest to the middle, the spot where you stand with your family, are the same ones who are your biggest champions! They are the people who are your biggest cheerleaders, your strength, your inspiration, your confidantes, and maybe even your mentors. These are the special people who always see you 'for you,' flaws, imperfections, and all, and they still love you! They are the ones who allow you to be yourself all the time. They don't want anything from you, but they do want things for you—like happiness, health, success, love, and joy. These persons don't compare themselves to you, and you don't feel the need to compare yourself to them either. You drop the veil around them and get to be yourself, and that is the value in the relationship!

Those persons in your outer circle may include some neighbors, friends of friends, acquaintances, and even a handful of toxic relatives whose caustic approach to life might threaten your journey's progress. There's a reason you keep them at more of a distance. It may be self-preservation and that's perfectly fine. When we allow people to move into our inner circle, it is a privilege to come closer, so it's acceptable to be selective about who we let in!

. . .

Even more important than those in your inner and outer circle are those at the nucleus of your circle. The core of all you do, and all you hold dear, are those persons who stand in the nucleus of your circle. Above all, protect those persons, shield them, value them, and hold them in the highest esteem, at all costs. These are the people who are on your team!

You and your spouse are both on an entrepreneur's journey, just like you're side-by-side in life walking through things together. Maybe, in the beginning, you didn't realize what it was going to look like, or feel like, or how much it was going to take to make it work, but you're in it now. For better or for worse, you're in it—together. Just like in all areas of your life, both you and your spouse must have some ground rules for how you'll each manage your parts in the entrepreneurial journey.

As hard as it is, take the 'me' and the 'my' out of the equation and focus on the other side of things. Stand back and look at what your partner is trying to do. Find compassion for what he or she might be going through and try to empathize. Your partner feels your frustration and knows that you may feel uneasy and scared about the future. This reality can also cause added stress and resentment to an already tenuous situation. The worst thing is for your spouse to feel as if you are against him or her and not on the same team. The last thing you want is for your spouse to feel alone, unappreciated, and unimportant. This only serves to widen the divide between you.

Again, setting expectations is important and communication is equally as critical. Agree to talk to each other without raw emotion, even when sharing your feelings. Keeping the lines of communication is much easier than trying to bridge a wide gap later if things have gone unsaid and avoided. But remember that it's not always 'what you say' but 'how you say it' that matters most!

Decide on the best time to talk to your spouse. Know what points you want to express and what outcome you hope to achieve. Remind yourself that it's not about laying blame or pointing fingers, but that your goal is to facilitate progress in your joint journey. Go into a conversation not with a list of points of how your spouse is failing you, but rather with what you'd like to see happen following your talk. This will keep the conversation on a positive note and it'll lessen the likelihood that your spouse will take the defensive and erect a protective wall that's impenetrable to you.

Most importantly, after you've shared your thoughts or concerns, ask then what your spouse thinks about how you see things. Chances are, he knows he needs to be more present and he also knows that he spends a lot of time on the business. He probably doesn't like it either! If you've presented your feelings in a factual, non-emotional way, his reactive response will be more open and honest. The scenario will allow you both to be on the same side as you consider how to rectify the situation.

Be ready to hear honest feedback though and prepare to hear his perspective on the state of things, just as he listened to yours. Let him speak, without interruption, without defense, and with no negative body language. Perhaps he feels you should be more supportive and understanding of his long hours and intense drive to succeed. It's perfectly normal for him to feel the weight of the world on him to provide for his family. At the very core of his long hours and exhaustive efforts lies the truth—that he does it because he loves his family. Most likely, he also wants to be more present, both physically and emotionally.

Ask how you can help. Get in, roll up your sleeves and pitch in as you can to remove some of the burdens that are on your spouse. Sometimes just knowing someone is helping serves to lessen the stress we feel because we envision someone carrying some of the burdens and sharing it. Perhaps getting involved in some way will allow for more quality time. It will also open your eyes to how your spouse spends his time, the hours he puts in, and how hard he works to provide for the family you and he share. In time, 'his thing' will likely feel like 'our thing' and you'll both feel closer as a result!

No matter the topic of conversation or the issue at hand, find out what your spouse needs from you. Simply hearing "What can I do help?" removes some of the weight from our spouses' shoulders. It also puts us on the same team as we work toward a common goal. Above all, when communicating, hear each other. To ensure you've heard what your spouse needs, verbally reiterate what you've heard. Just like positive affirmations, this helps to 'put it out into the universe' as a tangible tool that'll help both of you!

# MARRIED TO THE BUSINESS

DOES IT SOMETIMES feel like there's a third person in your marriage? Do you occasionally even get the feeling there's a mistress who takes your spouse's time and attention? Are you lonely more often than not? Do you gaze longingly at couples and wish your spouse was with you too? Does your spouse sometimes seem distracted, distant, and as if he's thinking about something else?

**Congratulations! You are married to an entrepreneur!**

First, know that this is a normal 'side effect' of being married to an entrepreneur. Second, rest assured that you're not overbearing, selfish, or even losing your mind! And lastly, know that you're not alone in your feelings.

It's normal to want to be with your spouse and to want to share things with him. After all, that's why you married him.

• • •

Here are some of the most popular 'pain points' and common triggers that are frequently heard from entrepreneurs' wives:

*"I feel like I'm a single mom!"*

*"Even when we do try to spend quality time together,*

*his phone will inevitably ring and he then spends most of the time outside, talking business."*

*"He constantly checks his phone and I feel like he isn't present."*

*"He works twenty hours a day."*

*"It seems like he tunes me out and always thinks about business."*

*"By the time he gets home, we're done with dinner and bath time. I know the kids miss him too."*

*"I'm not sure it's worth it."*

*"This wasn't what I'd envisioned for our life!"*

. . .

Sure, the life of The Entrepreneur's Wife is fraught with frustrations, but it can also be an extraordinary journey at times. Like all things in marriage, the entrepreneurial life is something that must be discussed, arranged, compromised on, and shared. It's no secret that the health of the business dictates the lifestyle of the entrepreneur's family, and there are times when the business must be a couple's priority. This is a treacherous, sometimes even perilous, tightrope for the entrepreneur to walk. But just like 'time waits for no one,' neither do clients or their needs!

Especially in the early days of business, it is critical to do anything and everything to cater to clients and customers. It's been estimated that it costs five to seven times as much to replace a lost customer than to keep him in the first place. Customer acquisition is costly and time-consuming, especially for new start-ups. Therefore, business owners sometimes even place clients' needs ahead of their own. Statistics show that it's easier to sell new products to existing customers as a company builds goodwill and solidifies its reputation. It's also been shown that eighty percent of a company's future revenues will be provided by twenty percent of its existing customer base. Entrepreneurs know that their clients don't owe them their loyalty, but that it is earned, and they know it's up to them to earn it. Whether a company offers services or is product-driven, there is a human being at the other end every sale. That human has needs, feelings, opinions, and expectations that must be met. The entrepreneur knows that he must meet his clients' requirements, as well as the needs and requirements of his spouse. While he values both his clients and his spouse, he frequently finds himself doing a juggling act as he strives to balance all areas of his life!

To support your spouse and support the business that's the lifeblood of your family, decide what you can do to make things easier and less stressful. Remember, if you're not part of the solution, you're probably part of the problem. Decide to work toward helping your spouse or your teammate. If he's got the support of his spouse, it'll be easier for him to take care of business and then get back to family matters.

We've all got our gremlins, those nagging, nit-picking voices that feed off our emotions until they boil to the top and finally spew like a long-dormant volcano. You know the ones… Over and over, they say, "When is it my turn? What about me? Aren't I important anymore?" Those nagging voices continuously pummel you and remind you of what your spouse should be doing, drawing attention to the fact that he's falling short. The gremlins justify your feelings and encourage your emotions to catapult and swell until you lose all control and the gremlins then take over on your behalf. Sound familiar?

The scenario is played out in countless entrepreneurial homes. You are not alone, nor is your husband alone either in his perilous predicament as he attempts to balance home, marriage, family, and business while shouldering the weight of his dual responsibilities. There are still just twenty-four hours in a day, but an entrepreneur has fit in everything into the same window of time as someone who's an employee and works nine-to-five.

Rather than becoming resentful and hopeless when your husband is called away, try to put yourself in his shoes, just for a minute. Imagine what it must be like to walk in his shoes and attempt to give of himself to everyone, even when he's spent and exhausted. Instead of seeing the business as an interloper that takes time away from your family, try and see it as a segment of your family that sometimes must receive attention because it provides support for the foundation of your family's life. Remind yourself that your spouse would prefer to spend time with you and your kids, but that he's got a responsibility to ensure the health of the company too.

Since the beginning of time, primitive man felt the responsibility to hunt and to provide for his family's sustenance. It's the same today, but the entrepreneurial husband just uses different tools and tactics. His identity, even his self-worth, is directly tied to his ability to provide. As the leader or head of his family, he carries with him an innate desire to 'do his job.' Providing a lifestyle is proof to him, and to the world, that he's doing his job. If he didn't love his family, then his need to provide wouldn't be so inherently powerful (But it's difficult for

The Entrepreneur's Wife to remember this, when her husband is still at the office at 8:00 pm, for the third night in a row!).

It's important to not only understand his mindset but also to make plans for how you'll handle 'the gremlins' that creep in and fan the flames of your emotions. Do some soul searching and create a plan for how to deal with situations that will inevitably arise. For instance, 'What do you do when you feel like the business is taking precious time away from you and your spouse?' It's natural to feel as if someone is to blame for taking him away, and since the business is at times a faceless imposition, it's easier to lay the blame on your husband. In truth, all this serves to do is to put more pressure on him. It drives a wedge between both of you and when you do come together, you'll spend your time arguing about how he always works and how he puts the business first, ahead of you. Sound familiar, too?

When an entrepreneur is trying to build a business, he works harder than ever before, and he puts in more hours than he ever expected he would. It's not that the business is more important than his spouse or his family, but it's because of his spouse and family that 'failure is not an option.' Whatever it takes, day or night, he will do to ensure the success of his business. But what happens to The Entrepreneur's Wife while he's giving his all and building the business?

The loneliness that can creep in can be overwhelmingly smothering. She may grow to see the business as the enemy, the thing he chooses over her. It can be a love-hate relationship, really. The wife's rational mind knows it's necessary for a business owner to invest time and energy into the business, especially when it's new, and yet she still misses her husband and craves time with him (This probably also sounds familiar.).

### So, what do you do?
### How do you find balance and security?

Embrace the fact that you married an entrepreneur. Wasn't it his big views, incredible dreams, and positive attitude that first attracted you to him? Try and remember those early days and how you loved his energy and his exuberant spirit. Think about how his passion and zest for life virtually seeped from his pores and made you want to be with him! It's these things that make him who he is in the world. It's these traits that make him different and unique.

Being The Entrepreneur's Wife means that you are different too. Maybe you didn't realize what your life was going to look like, or feel like, even how much it was going to take, but you're in it now. You're knee-deep in the entrepreneurial life, for better or for worse, and it's a reflection and a result of what the two of you build together. This is another time when it's important to stop comparing 'your normal' to 'everyone else's normal.' It will never look the same, and it will never feel the same, but that's because entrepreneurs are different—and different can be great!

Recognize that you are different, and so you must embrace a new normal—your normal, the normal that you create, and the normal that works for you and your family. Try and remove yourself from the equation, just for a minute, and look at what he is trying to do and why he's trying to do it. Try to get a better perspective and find compassion for what he's going through as he tries to build a life for your family. There are days when things are unbelievably tough, and he must stand on his dreams and struggle to maintain focus. Entrepreneurs don't have supervisors, managers, or even human resources personnel that act as their cheerleaders. There's no one to pat entrepreneurs on the back or to give them affirmation and feedback. An entrepreneur's position can be a lonely place at times, especially during the especially hard times. These are the times when The Entrepreneur's Wife can be his asset and the one person that stands with him, supports him, and shares his burdens.

Sure, you're frustrated at times, and he feels your frustration. That can be uncomfortable, even scary, for him. It can also cause unnecessary stress and resentment. The last thing you want is for him to feel like you're against him, especially during the tenuous, uncertain times. When it feels to him like the world is against him, it's The Entrepreneur's Wife's responsibility to stand beside him, tall and strong, as his biggest cheerleader and his sole support.

But rather than just offering emotional support, take it a step further and ask how you can help. Think about the early days of your relationship when it felt great to be 'the two of you against the world.' Let him know you're still in it and with him, but take another step and get in where you fit in. Depending on your own abilities and experience, you may be able to offer some relief by handling clients, overseeing quality control, billing customers, collecting receivables, creating a new marketing campaign, or just 'being the face of the company' and networking to retain current clients and secure new ones.

The benefits, however, will not only be to your spouse and to the company. Getting involved with the business will allow for more quality time with your spouse, a huge perk to The Entrepreneur's Wife. Your extra help will provide relief to your overburdened spouse, but it will do several things for you too. It will give you an inside glimpse into to all he does. You'll see firsthand how he juggles the business and all his overlapping responsibilities, and you'll gain an understanding of 'why he does all he does.' Instead of seeing the business as an interloper or a demanding mistress, you will most likely start to see it as the vehicle that will take your family to its goals. Instead of feeling like a passive passenger, just along for the ride, you will begin to feel like you and your spouse are driving toward your dreams!

Maybe you'll decide that 'his thing' can also be 'our thing,' just another facet that you share in life. Remember your dreams and how good it felt to share them together as you looked toward the future that you both wanted to build. Spend some time reminiscing on why you both agreed to start on the journey. It will refocus your outlook and help you to regain perspective. Sometimes entrepreneurs' lives are so full and busy, insane even at times, that it's hard to remember why they started the journey in the first place. Bring it all back into focus and remind yourselves of 'the end game' and what you want to achieve. What does it look like? What is your vision of success? Is your spouse's vision also the same? One shared vision is big. Dreaming together is HUGE! Working toward a dream means you'll get there faster, and even stronger, than when you began the journey!

Becoming involved in the business may not be for everyone, or for every marriage, and that's okay. We're all different, so it's important to do what works for ourselves and our marriages. Finding security, however, is something we all seek. Getting involved in the business can provide a sense of security as both your spouse and you work toward common goals. It can lessen the burden that he once shouldered on his own. It can refocus your dreams and provide a sense of 'togetherness' as you both take on the world 'as a unit.'

**There is a sense of security in all that, but what if 'working together' won't work for your marriage?**

There are several options that may still work to provide the sense of security that you seek. First, The Entrepreneur's Wife can still be supportive, still be a cheerleader, and still share in his dreams from the sidelines. Becoming an active, integral part of the business might not be for everyone. But being 'part of the team' is still a viable option. Depending on your spouse's business, this may look different for different people. Offering support might mean handling more responsibilities at home, sharing in some of his 'husband duties,' or simply leaving him a warm plate of dinner when he walks in the door. Remember that you're both a part of the team. Each of you can lessen the load on the other by doing even simple things that make life easier for that person.

Some wives find the security they seek by pursuing their own endeavors, either entrepreneurial or otherwise. This doesn't mean you're not 'part of the team,' but just that you're nourishing your own soul and fulfilling your spirit so that you can be a solid, contributing teammate in the end. There's a sense of empowerment that's found by learning something new and doing new things. Whether this means starting a business of your own, taking a class, volunteering, or becoming involved in a passion project, you'll come away feeling renewed and fulfilled. The result will make you a stronger teammate in the end. So, get involved—either in the business or in your own endeavor!

# 14
# USING TRAVEL TO GET AWAY & COME TOGETHER

I T'S NO SECRET that travel offers endless benefits to people but travel especially provides extraordinary benefits to entrepreneurial couples. First, just the opportunity to get out of the usual, predictable surroundings provides a fresh perspective, both personally and professionally. Standing back from our lives and looking at them from a new vantage point gives us a chance to reflect on why we do what we do! And let's face it, most of us are excited about the opportunity to travel with our spouse, even if it's primarily for business. Entrepreneurs are used to juggling dual responsibilities, and this skillset works perfectly when travel possibilities arise.

Setting expectations, long before the trip's departure, ensures that everyone's needs are met during the holiday. Consider the fact that the entrepreneur has a primary responsibility during the trip and until that's been met, it must be his focus. While he's busy making sales calls, networking, calling on accounts, or speaking at a venue, this provides the perfect opportunity for The Entrepreneur's Wife to get in a little 'me time.' Depending on the destination, this might include an afternoon at a hotel spa, some uninterrupted shopping time, sunbathing by the pool, or simply walking around and sightseeing in a new locale. He will feel comfortable that you're enjoying your time while he takes care of his responsibilities and you'll enjoy having time to renew and refresh, and you'll both enjoy coming together at the end of the day.

Keep in mind that he needs time to recharge his batteries too, especially since he's been working during part of the trip. Be sure to build in time for him to have a little 'me time' of his own. A little deep-sea fishing or a round of golf can do wonders for a busy entrepreneur, and he'll appreciate that you realize he needs—and deserves—the time for himself.

But the point of accompanying your husband on a business trip is so that you'll be able to sneak in some 'couple time' too. Before the trip begins, discuss your intentions and expectations. This ensures there are no gray areas and no unmet needs or hurt feelings. Entrepreneurs and their spouses must always make the most of their time and there's no value in wasting even an hour during a trip, whether it's for a week or just a weekend!

All trips have highs and lows. Anyone that has ever traveled with their spouse to an event or on business knows how emotionally taxing it is, not only individually, but for the relationship as well. It's not just the act of traveling, or even being out of our usual locales, that brings a sense of exhaustion. It's also not just the lack of sleep and the uncertainty of being in a new environment that is tiring. When traveling for business, the entrepreneur must always be on his 'A Game'—all day, every day. Be aware of this and recognize that your entrepreneurial spouse will have this extra weight on him, coupled with the purpose of the trip and the fact that he's concerned about how his wife feels during the trip too. Discuss these things beforehand. Decide on whether you'll meet for lunch during his workdays or if you'll get together for coffee between break-out sessions if he's got time.

Setting intentions and expectations ensures you'll both make the most of your time while on the trip.

Ask your spouse how you can best support him during the trip. He may need for you sometimes to be 'hands on' during part of an event; he may ask that you accompany him to a business dinner, or even befriend the spouses of his colleagues, or he may simple need for you to be there as his quiet source of support. While you want for your marriage to benefit from time spent together on the trip, there's also immense opportunity to deepen your marital bond by 'putting him first' and 'offering support' however best suits his needs.

Sometimes life is about him, sometimes it's about us, and sometimes it's about both of us, as a couple. Realize that most times, it's not an equal disbursement of attention and focus. When he needs to be the focus, facilitate his needs, and when your needs require attention, he'll be there for you. In marriage, it's always 'give and take.' For entrepreneurial couples, there's always that added dimension of 'the business' and the 'needs of the business,' so it's important to acknowledge and nourish that dimension at times, just as the business nourishes the lifestyle you and your family enjoy.

Travel always brings with it many opportunities for growth. It makes us step out of our comfort zones, try new things, talk to new people, and embrace the fact that the world is a gigantic place to be explored and savored. Travel always puts our lives into perspective and always changes the traveler in some way. The 'souvenirs' collected last a lifetime!

For couples, there's a sense of adventure in discovering new things together and in new places. Making memories in new places is exciting and special, almost like it was in the 'early days of dating.' Broadening our horizons reminds us that there are many people in the world, all dealing with their own issues and trials. It also shows us that there are people out there whose struggles are bigger than our own and conversely, we too sometimes see people who are doing better than we are, so we come away feeling inspired to reach higher. The effects of travel are different for everyone. Our unique observations and reactions are based on our personal pasts and experiences and on where we are in our own life's journey.

Business travel can be very beneficial, though it's a little different in some ways. It can be mentally draining and physically exhausting at times. This is because so much preparation goes into a trip, even before we embark on it. Just the physicality of travel is tiresome, never mind dealing with different time zones, schlepping our luggage, checking into hotels and coordinating meetings at our destination. And then, once we're at the conference, meeting, or corporate venue, we're 'still working.'

For these reasons, good health is more important than ever for both the entrepreneur and The Entrepreneur's Wife. Common sense things like eating well, drinking plenty of water, and getting enough sleep allow us to function optimally, so we'll make the most of our travels. Realize that both of you may feel irritable at times, due to the stress of travel, time zone differences, and schedule constraints. Instead of becoming overwhelmed and lashing out during times of travel stress, recognize it and let it go so you can make the most of the time you've got together. Realize that while traveling, 'life still happens,' and some things are out of your control. You and your spouse are a team though, so nothing can ruin your 'together time' unless you allow it!

If one person goes to an event and gets motivated, and then comes home and his spouse is not on the same level of inspiration, it is a little bit of a buzz kill, sort of like running full-force into a brick wall. This dynamic can separate a couple and deflate all the motivation that one of them found in the event. Just as couples share other facets of their life, they can also share the excitement, motivation, and connections found during travel. This makes traveling more fun because a couple can discuss the people they met, new viewpoints, exciting ideas, and dreams for their future. Many times, this opens an opportunity for brainstorming and collaboration that wouldn't exist if just one person had been present at an event. It's another opportunity to 'be on the same team' and 'be together on the journey.'

• • •

*We recently returned from an amazing trip to Canada during which Matt spoke about e-commerce at a marketing event. Traveling with Matt is fun and exciting. We love traveling together. Before we even left our home, I decided to make a conscious effort to make this trip about my husband and what he needed. Since Matt was to speak, I knew I'd be on an emotional rollercoaster of uncertainty and self-doubt, so I recognized this and vowed to not let it hinder my trip or Matt's experience. What my husband needed was for me to just be there and to support him with his endeavor. He needed for me to be 'the giver' this week, and for me to not need much in return. I was fine with that because he supports me when I need it too. Our trip was awesome, Matt did a great job at the event, and we went home feeling closer and more fulfilled as a result.*

*Did I execute my role flawlessly during our Canada trip? No, not really; I was good, but not perfect. There were many times during the week when I had to stop, breathe, and remind myself that 'it's not about me' right now. But I refocused my attitude and redirected my actions to support Matt and what he needed at the time.*

*For me, the most amazing part of the entire trip was watching my husband deliver his talk. Many years ago, Matt came to me and said, "I will be speaking on stage one day." I thought, "Okay cool," unable to see how his vision was going to eventually evolve and come to life.*

*Fast-forward to present day, and over the last few years, Matt has spoken all over the world. But his Canada talk was different. I was in the room, and it was a talk that he had not before given. I got the privilege to see how people received him and absorbed his message. I watched in awe, and with pride, as he was doing it! He was being the person he had worked so hard to become.*

*The moment was somewhat surreal, and I was full of emotion and bursting with pride. I was so emotional, in fact, that when we went back up to our hotel room, after he'd spoken, I cried. It was not just a 'subtle tear-up' during which I quietly shed a tear, not at all—I cried like a baby, overwhelmed with emotion that my husband had dared to dream and that he'd gone after what he wanted, and had created a life he loves (This is also why, when Matt is on-stage, that he banishes me to the back of the room. I'm a proud wife and seeing him zestfully live his dream makes me cry, which in turn, also makes him cry. So, no front seat row for this girl.).*

*Although my intention on our trip was to be focused on Matt and his needs, I still received some great messages and made some awesome friends in the process. Prior to our trip, we agreed we'd go there for a reason, and as a result, we both came away feeling enriched, energized, and motivated! It's a unique feeling that no tropical vacation can ever provide!*

*Matt and I have a mantra when traveling. We say, "We are either going to a venue or a place to hear a message or to give a message, and sometimes both." Going into our Canada trip, we were cognizant to be open to all possibilities and we both set our intentions. This ensured expectations were met and that we both got what we needed from the experience. The trip was an experience that will not soon be forgotten.*

· · ·

Busy entrepreneurs must grasp any opportunities to mix business and pleasure. Sure, 'all play' vacations are important too, but the health of the business relies on nurturing it, so we must sometimes 'sneak in some couple time' where we can! It's all part of the life on an entrepreneur and when his family embraces that fact, everyone is on board and everyone benefits! A business trip need not be 'all business' and couples must make the most of any opportunities to be together and experience new things. Travel is just one more opportunity to do this.

The wife of an entrepreneur must sometimes be willing to be focused on their entrepreneurial spouse and his needs. This scenario will happen many times during the entrepreneurial couple's journey. It does not mean ignoring or invalidating our own feelings, but rather taking the focus and temporarily redirecting it. When entrepreneurs take chances or risks or put themselves out there to be judged and critiqued, they need a special kind of support. The Entrepreneur's Wife is that safe place on which they need to rely.

Make sure you take care of yourself before a trip and during your travels. This is part of your responsibility as a teammate. Read books, meditate, go for walks, go to the spa, take long showers, pray, have sex, do something that fills your soul and your love tank. When someone needs a lot from you, it pulls from your energy, both emotionally and physically, so don't allow your energy to deplete or else the results will affect your performance as a teammate. You must make sure you are running on a full tank to be able to wrap yourself around everything. This also ensures that you'll be able to optimally support your spouse and his goals.

Restoring our souls and reigniting our passions through travel sends us home ready to take on the world! Making new memories in the process only enhances our relationship and the overall health of our marriage.

*"Life is an echo. What you send out, comes back. What you sow, you reap. What you give, you get. What you seen in others, exists in you."*

—Zig Ziglar

# 15
# MAKING THE DREAM A REALITY

T HERE ARE MANY examples I can give of things that we dreamed of in the beginning of our journey that have come to life and become realities. Matt and I envisioned and spoke about our dreams, put action behind our thoughts, and put our words into motion, and today we stand together, making it happen, changing lives, and living our life on purpose and on our own terms. Sure, it's been scary and tenuous at times, but it's also been greater than we could have ever imagined! The best part of our journey has been that we made it together, side by side, navigating the bumpy roads and hairpin turns, but also stopping to savor the scenery and make memories along the way.

We've learned about ourselves and about each other. Because of our journey, we've been made to dig deep, and sometimes dig in as we'd never had to do. We've faced obstacles, tackled seemingly insurmountable odds, figured things out, and worked our ways through all sorts of trials. When one of us felt that we couldn't go on, the other picked up the slack. When one of celebrated a victory, the other was right there, cheering and applauding.

Two of anything is always stronger than one, and that's what we've learned during our journey. We've also learned the importance of dreaming together and of 'choosing to find the magic' in life. Our journey continues today, and we still choose to do these things. They enrich us, fulfill us, and continue to bring us closer.

It's easy to become complacent and comfortable, and it's fine to linger in that state, but just not for too long. Entrepreneurs are a special breed. They thrive on challenge, and they seek new discoveries and bigger goals. Being with an entrepreneur is exhilarating and motivating. Being married to a big dreamer is infectious. A lot of times my husband just needed a partner to dream with and to share his visions. It is an amazing feeling when the things you and your spouse dreamed about together, so many years ago, start to come to fruition. It's empowering and exciting at the same time! 'Thinking big' seems somewhat like a cliché ideal, but when you are married to an entrepreneur, you must bust through all the glass ceilings. Big actions come from big thoughts, and the sky's the limit for a true entrepreneur!

Each of us is a different person than the person we were last month, last year, and even ten years ago. We're all a summation of all we've done and all we've experienced. Fortunately, we can choose to embrace the good and let go of the bad, but still take with us all the lessons we've learned along the way. One of the biggest lessons Matt and I have learned is that 'change is okay' and not to fear it. Change doesn't always mean something negative is on the horizon, but rather it means opportunity awaits. It's easy to become complacent, and when a change occurs, it sometimes feels unnerving. It can rattle us, startle us, and even frighten us because it brings with it 'the unknown.' Rather than becoming uneasy about new things, choose to 'see the glass as half-full.' Embrace the possibilities that await and decide how to instill energy into that change and use it to propel you forward in your journey!

Changes 'change us' too, and this can be a great thing. Change always leads to new opportunities, insights, and experiences that lend value in so many ways. Look at change as a sign that progress is on the horizon! It's nothing to be feared. It should be embraced, even invited!

Sometimes we can't control change. We can, however, decide how we will respond to change. Decide not to waste energy ruminating about or wallowing in sorrow when change comes around. Grab it, embrace it, and steer it in the direction that best supports your overall goals! Recognize that you're not a passenger, just along for the ride as 'change' drives your life. Where you go, what you do, and how you go through life are up to you! Realize that change also brings with it a new adventure and the chance to learn and grow.

In entrepreneurship, situations change daily, even hourly at times. There are the highest of highs and the lowest of lows. Yesterday's successes are in the past, and today is a new day, filled with promise and possibility. Because nothing stays the same, this can mean that finding the security in life is at times challenging. Being prepared to welcome change means being able to embrace it and adjust with it so that we can ride the waves of change to new, better things!

Look at change not as a 'noun,' something stagnant and motionless that stalls your progress. Change is a 'verb,' something that will move you along your journey and take you to something better. It's the vehicle that encourages us to get out of our comfort zones, do more, and be more in this life. With change always come endless possibilities!

Decide to embrace change, wrap your arms around it, and infuse it with a positive and a welcoming heart, and then 'hang on tight' for where it'll take you! Water must flow, or else it becomes stagnant and a pond scum grows on its surface. Life is the same. It must continue to flow, move, and change, so we don't become stagnant and too comfortable.

Another important lesson that I've learned as The Entrepreneur's Wife is to connect with other entrepreneurs' spouses, both to get support and to lend support. Each of us has something to give, to share, and to teach, and each of us benefits from what others share with us too. Being around the right people is crucial to the success of this unique journey. Our issues and concerns are different from those of others, but our rewards and gifts are different too, and for that, we are grateful. There is power and strength in being around like-minded people who enjoy making their own success! Make sure you surround yourself with people who support you and who give you positive vibes and inspiration. These are the same people who stand beside you in the good times and are also right there with you in the tough times.

With our fast-paced lives and never-ending obligations, it's easy to get bogged down and to forget why we do what we do in this crazy life. Entrepreneurs have great visualization skills that allow them to envision their success and the path they'll take to get there. Vision boards are another great way to create a tangible picture of our goals for the future. Psychological studies have even shown that our brains 'remind us and encourage us' to do what we regularly envision. Athletes and business professionals alike often use visualization techniques as part of their regimen, and while they have different goals, the results are often the same. That's because 'seeing is believing' and 'when we see it, we can achieve it!'

A vision board reinforces why we do what we do, and it inspires and motivates us to work toward the goals on our board. Creating a vision board can be as simple or elaborate as you'd like to make it. You can make one joint vision board that depicts the goals of you, your spouse, and your family, and you can also do a single, solo board that has your personal goals on it.

To create a vision board, think about what you'd like in this life. Do you desire a huge, new home in an exclusive neighborhood? Have you always wanted to own a certain sports car or luxury vehicle? Would you like to take a lavish European vacation? Do you have personal goals of losing a few pounds and becoming physically fit? Have you always wanted to learn how to speak a new language? Would you like to learn how to snow ski or scuba dive? Are you an adrenaline junkie who would like to skydive or perhaps climb Mount Everest? All these things if they appeal to you are things that could go on your vision board. Look online or thumb through magazines to find photos that depict your goals in life. Print and cutout photos that appeal to you and that support the visions you have for your future and then affix them to a large board. This can be a fun way to dream and plan for your future with your spouse and even with your kids. And what better lesson to teach your children than how to dream, create goals, go after them, and make them a reality?

Finding a new form of security was another big lesson that I learned during my journey. Nothing in life remains the same, and I had to find my footing on shifting sand and learn to be okay with it. The need for security is a strong desire for a lot of women. Without it, we often feel unsettled. When you're married to an entrepreneur, you must find a new kind of security. The steady paycheck doesn't exist a lot of times, especially in the beginning of the journey. With the lack of predictable income and residuals from investments, we can be left grasping for anything that remotely feels like safety. I had to learn to stay strong, trust my husband, and trust that 'together we are unstoppable' as we pursue our dreams!

While the entrepreneur is off building the business that will support his family, The Entrepreneur's Wife sometimes can feel left out and not like an integral part of creating the dream. Regular 'date nights' can help to foster a sense of closeness between a busy couple. Make a point to have a weekly 'date' and spend one-on-one time together. Set your intentions for these dates and allow your spouse to set his. During 'date night,' cell phones should be ignored, except for an emergency call from the babysitter. Agree that 'talk about business, finances, past arguments, or stressful topics' is entirely off limits during these dates. Use the time to reconnect and refocus. Talk, laugh, and just be together, without distractions or interruptions. Go to dinner, see a show, listen to a band, or just sit under the stars by the shore with a glass of wine. The time will, at the same time, relax and energize both of you, and leave you feeling connected, grounded, and united. You'll be ready to take on the world tomorrow!

Being okay with 'standing outside of the box' is for sure one of the biggest things I've learned over the years. I've had to find a new normal and fully embrace it, the 'normal' that Matt and I created together as we worked toward making our dreams a reality. In time, I've even come to love our 'new normal' and how we've made it work for our family!

In all things, even during the worst of times, choose optimism. Being optimistic seems simple, but when everything is stormy and gray, and your pessimistic side creeps in, you must strive to stay positive. It's a conscious choice that must be made, even on the most difficult of days! I've learned firsthand that an optimistic mindset is essential in this journey. There's no time for negativity and no reason for wallowing in unproductive thoughts and overwhelming emotions. They're merely wasted energies that could better be used to work toward the dreams and goals you've set for yourself!

Let's face it: Life is a balancing act. There is a lot that goes on in our everyday lives, and for entrepreneurs, our roles often merge, meld, and overlap, which makes the balancing act even more tedious at times. I had to learn that sometimes my husband and I do not have to have equal involvement as we each support our team. I've had to be okay with taking on more of our family life now and then, when my husband has a new launch or works on a big project, or during the times when he just needs space to create and plan. Learning to sometimes be okay with the lack of equality is key during the journey to making our dreams become realities.

It's important to remind yourself that you and your spouse are a team in all things. It's the two of you against the world; if this ship goes down, then you'll go down together, as a unit. I had to learn that we are not against one other, and that it is our differences that make us unique and valuable in this journey. We had to find the balance between what he needs and what I need, and then we had to communicate our needs in ways that the other one heard.

At times, early in our journey, it felt like we were fighting against each other, and as if we weren't on the same side, much less the same team. But we eventually learned that together we are stronger, and together we are better. It's much easier to remain focused on 'the dream' when there's someone beside us, working and striving toward the same goals! Being an entrepreneur is hard enough, with all the criticisms, judgments, and even at times, self-doubt. Resolve that 'the battle is out in the world,' but not within your home and not between you and your spouse. What resides within the walls of our home should be supportive, nurturing, safe, and cherished. We need to be able to remove our armor at home and feel completely secure, accepted, loved, and understood.

The Entrepreneur's Wife should learn to be gracious and supportive always, even in the aftermath of occasional bad decisions, failed attempts, or negative feedback from others. Every entrepreneur experiences some failures. It's a part of life and a rite of passage on the journey. When you're married to an entrepreneur, there will be some failed attempts during the process. Learn to bite your tongue, be supportive, and be gracious, even in those times. Taking risks is all a part of the life of an entrepreneur, and profit is the reward for that risk, even though it sometimes eludes us at first. It is hard to invest your life into building a legacy for your family, but it's even harder and lonelier when doing it alone. Decide that your entrepreneur won't be alone on the journey! Offer encouragement, support, and a reminder that you're still right there, a part of the team, win or lose!

Get involved in making the dream become a reality! I learned that I needed to participate, in some way, in the process. This 'participation' has varied for us over the years, depending on what the business needed at different times. One huge thing I've learned though is that not being involved creates a wide division, and that is unhealthy for the entrepreneurial family.

The Entrepreneur's Wife doesn't necessarily have to start being hands on in daily activities of the business but find how much involvement and interaction works for you and your spouse. Start there, discuss an approach, and become involved in working toward the dream!

I've also learned that's it's possible to effectively lead from the back. The Entrepreneur's Wife plays a vital role in the success of their family. Decide to be the cheerleader, the sounding board, and confidante to your entrepreneurial husband. Believe in him, even if he becomes weary and stops believing. Being behind the scenes, and wearing so many hats, as a mother, a wife, and a business partner, makes you an outstanding teammate that's vital to the team's overall success. You're a leader, even if when you're not in front of the pack because if you stop doing your part, the journey stalls and the dream becomes further away!

Entrepreneurs know it's 'up to them' to make things happen, both big and small. They must make things happen. They must affect change and implement methods. They know that 'the buck stops' with them, and they're perfectly willing to shoulder those responsibilities. It's in their nature. But successful entrepreneurs have learned that with change also comes the promise of something bigger, something new, or something exciting. Sometimes even the smallest change can lead us to huge benefits in the overall bigger picture.

Decide to 'be the change' that moves you forward in your journey. You, The Entrepreneur's Wife, are the backbone, the support system, the strength, and the glue that holds it all together. You and your contributions are very important and extremely necessary to the support, and even the success, of the entrepreneur's team. There are times when you are the team's Most Valuable Player!

Being married to an entrepreneur takes talent, strength, patience, and courage. I've learned a ton during our fourteen-year journey together, and I'm still learning. I know the journey isn't even close to being over, but I'm excited about what's waiting around the bend for us! Thanks to what I've learned, I now know how to navigate our journey.

Looking back, I smile because even though to the outside world our life probably seemed chaotic and crazy, we still held on to each other. One of the biggest lessons I learned over the last years is that we can choose happiness. We have the power to make a choice to be happy! When life isn't ideal, there are still options, and we can be a victim or a victor. Years ago, I didn't know why certain things were happening, but now I realize it was to teach us, to strengthen us, and to help us to relate to others who are going through similar struggles as they strive to turn their dreams into realities.

The prospect of change now excites me, and I look forward to what it may bring into our lives. The future holds endless possibilities, and with Matt at my side, we'll walk into our future together, eager and excited for what will come next! Many times, once people get used to the idea that change is happening, they also see that something even better is right around the corner. If Matt and I had known in 2008 that life would be so awesome in just a few years, then we'd have eagerly sped from Florida and hurried toward our future! Nearly a decade ago, while we were feeling tentative, uncertain, and nervous about our move and how our life would unfold, we really had all we needed, right there with us, as we drove through the rain toward North Carolina:

**We had our kids, each other, and our willingness to do whatever it takes to build the life of our dreams!**

# ABOUT AMY STEFANIK

AMY STEFANIK, CREATOR and Founder of The Entrepreneur's Wife, is an author and speaker with a passion for living the life of her dreams while sharing with others how to successfully do the same.

A health and fitness enthusiast, Amy was born and raised in Florida. She resides today in Waxhaw, North Carolina with her husband and children.

Learn more about Amy Stefanik, schedule her for an event, ask a question, or connect with her for inspiration at TheEntrepreneursWife.com.

**To keep in touch and for more resources from the book visit tewbook.com**

# MOTIVATE AND INSPIRE OTHERS!

**"Share This Book"**

**To Place an Order Contact:**

support@theentrepreneurswife.com

# THE IDEAL PROFESSIONAL SPEAKER FOR YOUR NEXT EVENT!

Any organization that wants to develop their people to become "extraordinary," needs to hire Amy for a keynote and/or workshop training!

## To Contact or Book Amy To Speak:

## support@theentrepreneurswife.com

# Morgan James
# Speakers Group

We connect Morgan James published
authors with live and online events
and audiences who will benefit
from their expertise.

Printed in the USA
CPSIA information can be obtained
at www.ICGtesting.com
JSHW022339140824
68134JS00019B/1583